Beyond the Bean Seed

Beyond the Bean Seed
Gardening Activities
for Grades K-6

Nancy Allen Jurenka
and
Rosanne J. Blass

1996
Teacher Ideas Press
A Division of
Libraries Unlimited, Inc.
Englewood, Colorado

TEACHER IDEAS PRESS
A Division of
Libraries Unlimited, Inc.
P.O. Box 6633
Englewood, CO 80155-6633
1-800-237-6124

Production Editor: Stephen Haenel
Copy Editor: Susan Brown
Proofreader: Lori Kranz
Design: Stephen Haenel and Michael Florman
Layout: Michael Florman

Library of Congress Cataloging-in-Publication Data

Jurenka, Nancy E. Allen, 1937-
    Beyond the bean seed : gardening activities for grades K-6 / Nancy Allen Jurenka and Rosanne J. Blass.
      xiv, 196 p. 22x28 cm.
      Includes bibliographical references (p. 163) and index.
      ISBN 1-56308-346-9
      1. Children's gardens. 2. Gardening--Experiments. 3. Botany--Experiments. 4. Botany--Study and teaching--Activity programs.
5. Teaching--Aids and devices. I. Blass, Rosanne J., 1937-   .
II. Title.
SB457.J87 1996
372.3'57--dc20   96-10790
                                                                     CIP

Contents

"From as far back as I can remember, I've been fiercely independent. I first learned the importance of making choices when at age seven I began to tend my own garden. What my garden taught me is how inspiring it is to decide things for oneself. I pored over Burpee's seed catalogues, trying out different varieties of lettuce and zinnias; I had some great successes and an equal amount of duds. I tended not to dwell on the crops that never broke ground or the tomatoes that rotted green on the vine. What I most vividly remember were the rewards: the exhilarating sensation of running out the kitchen door in the early-morning light before breakfast, with dew still on the grass, dodging spiderwebs, running barefoot to see what was cooking in my precious garden. I was the youngest serious gardener in town, and I felt grown-up."

Alexandra Stoddard, *Making Choices*
(New York: William Morrow, 1994, p. 21)

Introduction

Purpose

This is a book about books, in particular children's books related to gardens and gardening. The purpose of this book is to connect gardening with literacy and children's literature. It is written for adults who garden with children: classroom teachers, horticulturists, arboretum and botanical garden educational directors, librarians, parents, 4-H club leaders, leaders of Cub Scouts, Boy Scouts, Brownies, Girl Scouts, and Campfire Girls, Bible school teachers, Master Gardeners, Cooperative Extension Agents, gang prevention workers, social workers, nature and garden center teachers, home school parents, community and urban garden leaders and volunteers, retired people, and camp counselors. It is written to provide them with ideas for using children's books, language arts, and creative activities within a gardening setting.

History

Gardening and learning have been partnered for centuries. Cicero stated, "If you have a garden and a library, you have everything you need." It was Johann Amos Comenius, a Moravian bishop writing in 1632, who proclaimed that every school should have a garden and that children should be allowed to investigate the plants, soil, and animal life there. Comenius—known as the father of modern education for his belief that education was for all, not just the rich and privileged—urged teachers to connect the experiences that children had with gardening with reading and writing. He wrote that words should always be taught in combination with objects (Marturano 1994).

Johann Heinrich Pestalozzi, an eighteenth-century education philosopher, advocated the notion that children should examine objects from nature and then write about their observations. He encouraged teachers to bind the children's stories into books, an idea that is still in use (Marturano 1994).

Friedrich Froebel, founder of the modern-day kindergarten, insisted that most of the children's time in school be spent gardening. Froebel, writing in the early 1800s, foreshadowed today's integrated curriculum when he called teachers' attention to what he called budding points, those settings such as a meadow or garden that would lead to opportunities to study scientific principles such as light, color, or pollination (Marturano 1994).

A forward-looking educator, John Dewey stated in 1916:

> Carried on in an environment educationally controlled, [gardening activities] are means for making a study of the facts of growth, the chemistry of soil, the role of light, air, and moisture, injurious and helpful animal life, etc. There is nothing in the elementary study of botany which cannot be introduced in a vital way in connection with caring for the growth of seeds. Instead of the subject matter belonging to a peculiar study called botany, it will then belong to life, and will find, moreover, its natural correlations with the facts of soil, animal life and human relations. As students grow mature, they will perceive problems of interest which may be pursued for the sake of discovery, independent of the original direct interest in gardening—problems connected with the germination and nutrition of plants, the reproduction of fruits, etc. thus making a transition to deliberate intellectual investigations (p. 200).

Today, gardening with children while connecting it to literacy is a widespread practice in school and community. Organizations such as the United States Agriculture Department, the National Gardening Association, the National Science Foundation, the International Reading Association, Community Gardening Association, Federated Garden Clubs of America, and the American Horticulture Society actively promulgate its advantages for children.

Gardening is a dynamic springboard into the worlds of botany, nature study, ecology, art, color, design, folklore, and literature; into the worlds of history, geography, economics, cultural diversity, and mathematics; even into the worlds of music, drama, and dance. Gardening is the ideal curriculum integrator; it touches all commonly taught elementary school topics of study. Gardening also opens the door to career exploration—careers such as botany, horticulture, floristry, forestry, agriculture, soil science, ecology, geology, economics, politics, health and nutrition, pharmacology, city planning, recreation, and leisure.

In addition, gardening sets the stage for discovery learning, for questioning, for seeking answers and information, for problem solving, and creating hypotheses. It provides opportunities for observing, reflecting, recording, classifying, analyzing, synthesizing, reporting data, and communicating.

Finally, gardening provides opportunities to socialize the act of learning. Children who garden learn to work with each other, their parents, and other significant adults, to reach out to the community, and to work together to improve local conditions. Gardening engages boys and girls in authentic relationships with learning, with nature, with the environment, with civic agencies, and with adults and other children.

Experience-Based Literacy

It has long been held by educators that learning to read and write cut off from experience makes for a miserable and ineffective education. Readers and writers who are in the developing stage need experiences from which to formulate concepts and the labels for those concepts. They need experiences with which to make connections; upon which to think and reflect. These connected thoughts and reflections may then be turned into representations through drawing and writing. Reading one's own thoughts and then those of others becomes the final step.

To increase the literacy of your boys and girls you may want to to follow this sequence:

1. Begin with a gardening experience; it could be something very simple, such as planting a seed in a pot or rooting a cutting in water.

2. Discuss the experience. What was done? What did the children learn?

3. Have the children draw pictures with crayons or markers. The pictures should show their versions of what happened during the activity.

4. Either have the children dictate a recounting of the activity or write their own recounting. If the children do their own writing, be very accepting of their ways of expressing themselves in writing, including the manner in which they spell. Allowing the use of invented spellings encourages written production. Insisting on conventional spelling interferes with the free flow of ideas.

5. If the children say, "I don't know how to spell [a word]," tell them to scribble spell (make a scribble line at the place where the word would be) and to continue to put their thoughts on paper.

6. Have the children read the recounting to you or another person.

7. Collect and save the stories written or dictated by the children. Bind each child's stories into a book. Have the children read their stories from time to time.

Connecting writing to reading and vice versa is a powerful way to develop literacy; therefore, add the reading of a book related to the children's writing topic or current gardening interest. To support children's reading, you may want to use this sequence:

1. Find a related book that you think will be easy for the children to comprehend.

2. Allow the children to survey the book, looking at pictures, graphics, storyline, and chapter headings.

3. Ask the children, "What do you think this book is about?"

4. Ask the children, "What do you already know about _____?"

5. "What are some of the things you would like to know about _____?"

6. Say, "Read these pages to find out what the author tells you about _____."

7. Allow the children time to read the pages aloud or silently.

8. After the children have read the selection, ask "What did you learn?"

9. If the children come to an unknown word, tell them to skip the word and to read to the end of the sentence. Ask, "What words might make sense in this sentence?" Encourage several responses, including yours. By adding your choices, you model this figuring-out process for the children. Then ask, "Which one of our guesses matches the author's word?"

Other ways to help children read a book are:

1. Pair them with another child.

2. Read or have the book read to the children.

3. Make a tape recording of the book being read so the children may follow along.

4. Involve your youngsters in literature circles. Literature circles, described in *Creating Classrooms for Authors,* are small groups of children discussing a book that all have read (Harste, Short, and Burke 1988). The adult leader encourages discussion by asking a few open-ended questions.

As you begin to gather materials for the lessons described in this book, ask the librarian or media specialist at your public or school library or at your local arboretum, garden center, botanical or zoological gardens for assistance in collecting print and nonprint reference materials and in developing your students' basic reference skills.

Guidelines for Gardening

If you are just beginning to consider gardening with children, form a support system first. Form a planning committee to seek answers to these questions:

1. Where will the garden be located? It will need:

    At least six hours of sun.

    A conveniently located water source.

    To be out of the way of heavy foot traffic.

    To not replace a popular play area.

2. Who will prepare the site; do the rototilling?

3. Who will garden with the children?

   Consider retired people, Master Gardeners, volunteers, aides, teachers, older teens.

4. What is a reasonable adult-to-child ratio?

5. How will vandalism be prevented?

6. How will the garden be cared for over vacation periods?

7. Where will contributions of seeds, plants, and tools be obtained?

8. How can watering and weeding be kept to a minimum?

9. Will each child have a plot or will everyone work in a large common plot? Will you have a combination of both?

10. How will the produce be divided? Will the children have what they each harvested on a particular day, or will you collect every child's harvest into one common set and then divide it evenly among the children?

11. How will fund raising be handled? Do you need to learn how to write grant proposals?

12. Do you need permission from a governmental agency or private party? How do you get it?

Answers to these and other gardening-with-children questions may be found among these resources:

   Cooperative Extension Agents (county government pages in your phone book)

   Master Gardeners

   Botanical garden personnel

   Garden club members

   Science teachers

And these books:

Bremner, Elizabeth, and John Pusey. *Children's Gardens: A Field Guide for Teachers, Parents, and Volunteers.* University of California Cooperative Extension Common Ground Garden Program, 1990. Information about the availability of this book may be obtained from Common Ground Garden Program, University of California Cooperative Extension, 2615 S. Grand Ave., Suite 400, Los Angeles, CA 90007.

Get Ready, Get Set, GROW. A kit available from the Brooklyn Botanical Gardens, 1000 Washington Ave., Brooklyn, NY 11225.

Jaffe, Roberta. *The Growing Classroom.* Project Life Lab, 1982. Available from Project Life Lab, 809 Bay Ave., Suite H, Capitola, CA 95010.

Ocone, Lynn, with Eve Pranis. *The National Gardening Association Guide to Kids' Gardening.* John Wiley & Sons, 1990. Available from National Gardening Association, 180 Flynn Ave., Burlington, VT 05410.

Tilgner, Linda. *Let's Grow!* Storey Communications, 1988. Available from Storey Communications, Pownal, VT 05261.

Once you have a plan formulated, start digging and reap many benefits for children.

Organization of the Book

This book is divided into five sections. Chapter 1, "Getting Started," eases the hesitant adult leader into gardening with children as well as provides a classroom teacher with a beginning for September when school begins and most outdoor gardening ends (thus creating a dilemma). Chapters 2 through 6 describe plants, their parts and functions, and plant groups. Chapters 7 through 10 are sequenced from getting ready to garden to actual gardening. Chapter 11 encourages gardening groups to experiment with different types of gardens, especially city gardens.

You, the reader, will have your own ideas about organization.

Feel free to organize and sequence the lessons provided in *Beyond the Bean Seed* in ways that suit you and your situation. Because this book is written for a diverse readership, including Summer volunteers at a community children's garden, 4-H club leaders, classroom teachers, and horticulturists, readers may need to impose their own organization on the material.

If it is September and you are planning to make a Summer children's garden the culmination of a year's study, start with Chapter 1 and proceed lesson by lesson. If you are a gardening novice who doesn't know a sepal from a spade, start with Chapters 1 and 2, "Getting Started" and "Botany"; then pick and choose those lessons that fit your needs.

You may already have an established school or community garden and wish to expand your students' basic garden knowledge to ecology, social studies, famous people, or other garden-related studies. You will find appropriate sections that integrate gardening with other topics.

You may be an experienced gardener reading this book in the late Spring and you may be anxious to start gardening with children then and there. Begin with Chapter 7 and start digging.

Beyond the Bean Seed contains 55 lessons. Each lesson consists of:

A book-sharing time to start each lesson. Because one of the primary goals of this book is to lead children to books by the garden path, all the lessons begin with and are based upon a book. Share the book with your group. You can read the book or parts of the book aloud, showing the illustrations, or telling the story. You may also be able to obtain multiple copies of the book so that your children may enjoy the book on their own during a silent reading time. You may also enlarge the book into a Big Book format so it may be shared at one time with a group. Picture books that have a minimum amount of text adapt well to this method. You may not be able to find the lead book suggested. Use others listed in the "Read More About It" section or in the bibliography at the end of the book. Included with each book entry is a coded reference to the approximate grade level of the book: *P* equals primary, K-3; *P-I* refers to grades 2-4; and *I* refers to the intermediate grades 4-6.

A gardening activity based upon the book. This activity may last a few minutes or a few months. For long activities, you will need to remind the students about the book and gardening connection from time to time. It may be appropriate to incorporate the books from the "Read More About It" section during longer projects.

A language arts activity. This may involve speaking, listening, writing, reading, or a combination of some or all. Drama, poetry writing, book compiling, and journal keeping are often featured. When you wish to do this activity is best left up to you and your circumstances. It may best be done at the beginning, middle, or end of the gardening activity.

A creative activity. This may consist of creative thinking, dancing, painting, dramatic productions, puppet making, and party productions.

Most of these activities ask the adult leader to support the children as they reach out to the wider community either for assistance and resources, or to share garden products, knowledge, entertainment, or glad tidings. Sharing and giving away have a way of increasing a positive attitude toward self.

A treat. For most, but not all, the lessons, a treat recipe has been included. Arboretums and botanical gardens that have children's gardening programs contributed some of the recipes, which they offer to both children and volunteers to reward them for their hard work. You may wish to do the same.

A poem reference. Nearly every lesson contains a reference to a poem. Please take the time to find the poem or a substitute. Including poetry in each lesson gives your lesson a lift up and out of the grub work. Read the poem aloud to your group and copy it onto a chart for all to read and share. At your local library you will likely find the *Children's Poetry Index*, in which poems are listed by topic. Ask the children's librarian to help you. Be sure to tell him or her what you are doing—connecting children's gardening with children's literature. That way the librarian may be on the lookout for other appropriate poems for you.

Word play. The language of gardening is fun: full of puns, truisms, technical Latin-based vocabulary, wise sayings, metaphors, jokes, and riddles. Thus, gardening language readily lends itself to "Word Play," which is included in most, but not all, lessons.

Supplemental reading. To encourage further reading or to provide you with substitutes for the lead book, a "Read More About It" section is included with each lesson. The books included in *Beyond the Bean Seed* were chosen for their appropriateness to the lesson and their availability. All were found on the shelves of public and school libraries. Not all libraries will have all books, so we've listed lots of substitutes. As this book was written, it was easy to observe that libraries everywhere have tight budgets and that most gardening-related books have older copyrights. In defense of those older books, they have some of the best gardening advice, so hang on to them. The newer ones may be prettier but sometimes lack the substance of, say, Katherine Cutler's *The Beginning Gardener*.

Each lesson therefore consists of:

      a book and its synopsis,

      a gardening activity,

      a language arts activity,

      a creative activity,

      a treat,

      a poem,

      word play, and

      a list of supplemental books.

References

Dewey, John. 1916. *Democracy and education.* New York: Macmillan.

Harste, Jerome C., Kathy G. Short, and Carolyn L. Burke. 1988. *Creating classrooms for authors.* Portsmouth, N.H.: Heineman.

Marturano, Arlene. 1994. *The educational roots of garden-based literacy. GARDN Newsletter.* Vol. 1, no. 3 (Summer).

Chapter 1
GETTING STARTED

If you are hesitant about jumping into a full-blown gardening program, if you don't have a lot of time with the group with which you are working, or if you are a classroom teacher at the beginning of the school year in the Autumn and you are wondering how to begin to garden just when frost is imminent, this section is for you.

Begin with what is at hand. Let the plants on your windowsill blossom into garden-based literacy activities. Begin by featuring a plant of the week. Continue by taking your group on a nature walk around the block, down the road, or around the park or playground collecting stuff and creating a nature museum. When the weather becomes inclement create indoor gardens by growing kitchen gardens, by designing and planting windowsill gardens, or by growing plants in terrariums.

Use the "Getting Started" activities to establish a common purpose for questioning, oral discussion, and focused listening; for reading, writing, note taking, organizing, and reporting information; even for storytelling and small group or cooperative group activities. Some of the activities may serve as an introduction to other activities in this book, may be extended to activities based on the interests of your boys and girls, and will act as a springboard to the multifaceted world of gardening.

"Plant of the Week" may be done any time of the year and extended for as long as there is interest. "Collecting Stuff" is probably best done in the Autumn and most likely would take several days. "Garbage Gardens" may be done any time and may last as long as there is interest, but the unit will need at least two weeks so that plant cuttings and seeds will have time to take root. "Windowsill Gardens" and "Gardens Under Glass" may be done any time during the year. The intent of "Getting Started" is just that—to provide you, the adult leader, with easy entry into the world of gardening with children.

1.1 Plant of the Week

Holmes, Anita. *Flowers for You: Blooms for Every Month.* Bradbury, 1993. 48 pp. (I).

Twelve potted plants chosen for twelve months of bloom include Christmas and orchid cactus, both of which are tropical cacti. The introduction presents basic botany such as plant parts, environmental needs, and instructions for caring for plants. A plant chart shows plants, blooming seasons, such environmental needs as light, temperature, and humidity, and finally comments regarding care. This attractive book of blossoming plants is likely to appeal to children and provide an introduction to plant life and indoor gardening.

Gardening Activity

Feature a Plant of the Week

Begin with the plants on your windowsill by featuring a plant of the week. Early introduction of desert cacti or carnivorous plants is likely to engage the immediate interest of your youngsters.

You may borrow additional plants from others or invite boys and girls to bring plants from home. Extend your invitation to parents, community members, local garden clubs, and horticultural organizations. Some florists and garden centers will loan plants for a week of study.

Each week select a plant to feature. Along with boys and girls, generate questions such as the following to consider as you study your plant of the week.

1. What do we already know about this plant?

2. What do we want to know?

3. What is the geographic origin of this plant?

4. What is its native habitat?

5. Are stories, legends, or folklore associated with this plant?

6. Are there literary references or allusions to this plant?

7. Are poems, music, or dances associated with this plant?

Discuss these or similar questions, record children's answers, then use a variety of reference materials to research additional information about the featured plants. Ask the librarian or media specialist at your public or school library or at your local arboretum, garden center, or botanical or zoological gardens for assistance in collecting print and nonprint reference works and in developing basic reference skills of your boys and girls.

Allow children to work in pairs, small groups, or in cooperative groups to find and share information with the whole group. Summarize findings by making a two-column group chart using the headings "What We Have Learned" and "Questions We Still Have."

Language Arts Activity

Plant of the Week Journal

In your Plant of the Week journal, record information about each featured plant. Illustrate the journal with drawings, photographs taken by boys and girls, or pictures cut from garden catalogs or magazines.

Creative Activity

World Map of Featured Plants

Develop a world map showing the geographic origins of featured plants. Mount a world map on the wall. With push pins or transparent tape attach the names or pictures of featured plants to their countries or geographic areas of origin. As the world map develops, chart or graph featured plants with countries, geographic areas, or continents of origin.

Treat

Ice Cream Flower Pots

1 quart softened ice cream   green sprinkles
6 green straws   6 paper cups
fresh, artificial, or candy flowers

Spoon ice cream into paper cup. Stick a toothpick into the ice cream and slip a straw over it to make the stem. Sprinkle ice cream with green sprinkles. Slip a flower into the straw and serve.

Poem

Williams, Rosemarie. "Have You Thanked a Green Plant Today?" In *Lyrical Voices,* ed. Lincoln B. Young. Young Publications, 1979.

Word Play

Common plant names such as prayer plant, moses-in-the-bullrushes, or spider plant frequently describe characteristics of plants or refer to something they resemble.

Read More About It

Dietl, Ulla. *The Plant and Grow Project Book.* Sterling, 1993. 48 pp. (I).

Fenten, D. X. *Plants for Pots.* Lippincott, 1969. 128 pp. (I).

Lerner, Carol. *Dumb Cane and Daffodils: Poisonous Plants in the House and Garden.* Morrow, 1990. 32 pp. (I).

Pulver, Robin. *Nobody's Mother Is in Second Grade.* Dial, 1992. 32 pp. (P).

Robson, Denny, and Vanessa Bailey. *Rainy Days Grow It for Fun.* Gloucester, 1991. 32 pp. (P-I).

Soucie, Anita. *Plant Fun: Ten Easy Plants to Grow Indoors.* Four Winds, 1974. 126 pp. (I).

Zion, Gene. *The Plant Sitter.* Harper. 1959. 26 pp. (P) .

1.2 Collecting Stuff

Webster, David. *Exploring Nature Around the Year: Fall*. Messner, 1989. 48 pp. (I).

This book is one of a series of four that encourage readers to explore seasonal changes in the natural world. This book focuses on Fall whereas the others focus on Winter, Spring, and Summer. Select the book that corresponds with your season of use.

Pictures, diagrams, and readable text present information and activities. Fall explorations feature leaves, apples, seeds, soil, birds, and animals as well as the sky. The final project is to create a nature museum.

Gardening Activity

Gather and Create a Nature Museum

Open the world of nature study by encouraging children to explore their yards and garden beds, the countryside or a vacant lot, sidewalk cracks and parking lot fences. Encourage them to gather specimens such as flowers, seed pods, leaves, stems, branches, or weeds. Organize and display specimens according to the microenvironments in which they were found, i.e.: yards, garden beds, countryside, vacant lot, sidewalk cracks, and so on.

Language Arts Activity

Descriptive Labels

With your boys and girls generate a set of questions such as the following:

1. Where was it growing?

2. Under what conditions was it growing?

3. At what stage of growth is it?

4. What is it? (The best name children may give is "Jamie's" weed.)

Discuss the questions. Name and describe the specimens. Write descriptive labels and add them to the classroom display.

Creative Activity

Crayon Rubbings

Make crayon rubbings of specimens gathered by children by laying a sheet of paper over the specimen and rubbing with a crayon. Display crayon rubbings with the specimens and written labels.

Treat

Nature Walk Spicy Nuts

Beat together: 2 tablespoons water and 1 egg white. Add:

1/2 cup sugar	1/2 tsp. salt
1/4 tsp. cinnamon	1/4 tsp. ground
1/4 tsp. allspice	cloves

Mix well and add: 2 1/2 cups nuts

Spread mixture onto greased cookie sheet.

Bake at 250° for 1 hour.

Poem

Florian, Douglas. *Nature Walk*. Greenwillow, 1989.

Read More About It

Burnie, David. *How Nature Works:100 Ways Parents and Kids Can Share the Secrets of Nature*. Reader's Digest, 1991. 192 pp. (I).

Katz, Adrienne. *Naturewatch: Exploring Nature with Your Children*. Addison-Wesley, 1986, 128 pp. (I).

Kohl, Mary Ann, and Cindy Gainer. *Good Earth Art*. Bright Ring, 1991. 224 pp. (I).

Mitchell, Andrew. *The Young Naturalist*. Usborne, 1989. 32 pp. (I).

Shanberg, Karen, and Stan Tekula. *Plantworks*. Adventure Publications, 1991. (I).

1.3 Garbage Gardens

Handelsman, Judith F. *Gardens from Garbage*. Millbrook, 1993. 48 pp. (P-I).

For librarians, classroom teachers, and youth leaders who want to begin gardening with children but who don't want to go full-out with a 10′-x-12′ all-Summer garden, this may be just the book. Although it is written for children, adults will find plenty of ideas to use as they work with boys and girls.

Handelsman provides her readers with numerous clearly described projects that are simple and affordable—she is talking about garbage after all—and guaranteed to be successful. If you try the pineapple growing project, allow the pineapple top to dry out for a few days before planting and keep in mind that it can take up to two years to produce another pineapple. Other activities include the planting of wheat berries, yams, carrot tops, and avocado pits.

The sidebars of Handelsman's book contain fascinating vignettes about the legend, lore, and history of various plants, including the tomato, the potato, and garlic. Did you know that workers building the Egyptian pyramids went on strike to obtain a ration of garlic?

Gardening Activity

Growing Kitchen Scraps

Salvage kitchen or cafeteria scraps such as potato eyes or sprouts, carrot and pineapple tops, and citrus, apple, pumpkin, squash and avocado seeds to plant and grow your own garbage garden. While you plant and grow your garbage garden, collect and read tales about your kitchen scraps. You may wish to begin by planting bean seeds and exploring variations of "Jack and the Beanstalk" or by planting apple seeds and reading about Johnny Appleseed. Grow carrot tops upside down, serve carrot bread, and read "Why Carrots Are the Color of Flame" in Anne Pellowski's *Hidden Stories in Plants*. Plant raw peanuts, serve peanut butter sandwiches, and read about George Washington Carver. Growing kitchen scraps may generate interest in studying plant parts, seeds, or life cycles of plants and serve as an introduction to Chapter 2, "Botany."

Language Arts Activity

Create a Cookbook

Ask family members, friends, and neighbors for their favorite recipes using your garbage garden plants. Gather, record, and organize recipes into a cookbook. Identify the source of the recipe with the contributor's name.

Creative Activity

Invisible Ink

Provide your group with these directions:

Squeeze lemon juice into a bowl. Dip a brush into the juice and write a secret message on a piece of paper. When the juice dries, the message will become invisible; when the paper is held up to a lit lightbulb, the markings reappear.

Treat

Popcorn

Plant a few kernels of popcorn and pop the rest.

Poem

Walker, Lois. "Oats, Peas, Beans, and Barley Grow." In *Get Growing! Exciting Indoor Plant Projects for Kids*. Wiley, 1991.

Word Play

Jokes and riddles about plants may be found in Stephanie Johnson's *Tomatoes and Other Killer Vegetable Jokes and Riddles* (Doherty, 1992) or Bob Vlasic's *101 Pickle Jokes* (Pyramid, 1974).

Read More About It

Calhoun, Mary. *The Sweet Patootie Doll*. Morrow, 1957. 32 pp. (P). Illustrated by Roger Duvoisin.

Dietl, Ulla. *The Plant and Grow Project Book*. Sterling, 1993. 48 pp. (I).

Lindberg, Reeve. *Johnny Appleseed*. Little, Brown, 1990. 32 pp. (I).

Pellowski, Anne. "The Farmer and His Yams." In *The Story Vine*. Collier, 1984. 116 pp. (I).

Raferty, Kevin and Kim. *Kid's Gardening: A Kid's Guide for Messing Around in the Dirt*. Klutz, 1989. 87 pp. (P-I).

Walker, Lois. *Get Growing! Exciting Indoor Plant Projects for Kids*. Wiley, 1991. 102 pp. (P-I).

1.4 Windowsill Gardens

Bunting, Eve. *Flower Garden.* Harcourt Brace Jovanovich, 1994. 32 pp. (P-I). Illustrated by Kathryn Hewitt.

Kathryn Hewitt's glowing illustrations coupled with Bunting's rhyming text relate a contemporary urban story about a little girl and her father who plant a window box garden as a surprise birthday present for her mother.

Gardening Activity

Growing a Windowsill Garden

Create a windowsill garden by inviting boys and girls to bring seeds, seedlings, cuttings, and potted plants. Dig from the garden or buy bulbs for indoor forcing. Care for the potted plants. Watch the cuttings root, then plant them. Start your seeds in late Winter or early Spring. Creating a windowsill garden may serve as an introduction to Chapter 2, "Botany Lesson," or to 1.1. "Container Gardening."

Language Arts Activity

Poetry Writing

Use the two-line rhyming text of *Flower Garden* as a model. With children compose two-line stanzas to tell your own story of creating a windowsill garden.

Creative Activity

Box-Lid Gardens

Box-lid gardens are an alternative to planting seeds in Styrofoam cups or cartons. Box lid gardens provide the opportunity not only to plant seeds but to create miniature gardens and environments. Materials are simple and readily available: an assortment of boxes or box lids, pebbles, plastic, soil, and assorted garden-related materials.

1. Line a box lid with plastic.

2. Spread charcoal and pebbles on the bottom.

3. Spread potting soil on top of the pebbles.

4. Leave flat, or, for a contoured look, push the soil into sloping hills and valleys.

5. Plant grass seed and small plants.

6. Use stones, twigs, or moss to create the desired effect.

7. Place in a sunny window.

8. Water daily with a spray bottle.

9. Trim lawn with scissors and replace plants as needed.

(Directions for box-lid gardens were taken from *Responding to Literature: Activities for Grades 6, 7, 8* by Rosanne J. Blass and Nancy E. Allen Jurenka [Englewood, CO: Libraries Unlimited, 1991, p. 86].)

Treat

Flower Basket Cupcakes

Bake cupcakes and top with white frosting. Cut small paper doilies crisscross in center. Slip them over the bottom of each cupcake for a ruffled edge at the top. Attach pipe cleaner handles tinted with food coloring. Attach flower name cards.

Poem

de la Mare, Walter. "Seeds." In *Time for Poetry,* by M. H. Arbuthnot. Scott, Foresman, 1967.

Word Play

"Fresh as a daisy" and "fair as a lily" are two common similes.

Read More About It

Dietl, Ulla. *The Plant and Grow Project Book.* Sterling, 1993. 48 pp. (I).

Eckstein, Joan, and Joyce Gleet. *Fun with Growing Things: A Guide to Indoor and Outdoor Gardening for Kids.* Avon, 1991. 135 pp. (P-I).

Markmann, Erika. *Grow It! An Indoor/Outdoor Gardening Guide for Kids.* Random House, 1991. 47 pp. (P-I). Illustrated by Gisella Konemund.

Milord, Susan. *Kids' Nature Book: 365 Indoor/Outdoor Activities and Experiences.* Williamson, 1989. 158 pp. (P-I).

Wilkes, Angela. *My First Garden Book.* Knopf, 1992. 48 pp. (P-I).

1.5 Gardens Under Glass

Parker, Alice. *Terrariums*. Franklin Watts, 1977. 46 pp. (P-I).

   Three types of terrariums are described: tropical, woodland, and desert. In very clear, easy-to-follow directions, Parker leads the terrarium creator step by step through the process of constructing a pretty garden under glass. The concepts and technical terms associated with terrariums are printed in boldface and explained so that vocabulary development as well as indoor gardening practice is supported. The copyright may seem old to some; however, the seventies were the heyday of terrariums and this book is one of the best on the subject.

Gardening Activity

Making the Basic Terrarium

   Have on hand the following materials:

   large, clean wide-mouthed jars (check with cafeterias and restaurants)

   small rocks

   crushed charcoal

   plastic wrap

   squares of nylon

   potting soil

   hosiery material

   rubber bands

   Plants in 2" or 3" pots such as Norfolk pine, baby tears, peperomia, dwarf dracaena, strawberry begonia, Chinese evergreen, and mosses.

Provide your group with these directions:

1. If the jar is not clean, wash it thoroughly with hot soapy water. Rinse well.

2. Place about 1 inch of small rock at the bottom.

3. Place a piece of nylon material on top of the rocks.

4. Place a layer of crushed charcoal on top of that. Less than an inch will do.

5. Place a second piece of nylon hosiery material on top of the charcoal. It's important to have this barrier between the soil and the charcoal.

6. Add about 3 inches of commercial potting soil on top of these layers.

7. Plant about three plants. An old iced-tea spoon makes a good digging tool for this step.

8. Spritz the plants with water.

9. Cover the jar with plastic wrap, securing it with a rubber band.

Creative Activity

Imaginary Miniature Worlds

Have on hand the materials listed above. In addition, have miniature plastic people and animals, mirror shards, miniature toys, and other props. Say to your group the following:

"Now that you know the basics of terrarium building, what other kinds of places would you like to create? Are there storybook places that you could re-create with a terrarium? What kind of terrarium world could you create for books such as *The Secret Garden* or *Chess Dream in a Garden*, or characters such as Kermit or Bambi? Take a few minutes to think about it and then do it."

Allow time for your boys and girls to do the activity and then go on to the language arts activity described below.

Language Arts Activity

Miniature World Stories

After doing the creative activity, read or tell these directions to your group:

"You've created a miniature world with your terrariums. What would happen if the people and animal figures in your terrarium came to life? What adventures would they have in the land that you have created for them? Write a story about your terrarium world."

Treat

Treat in a Jar

In those 8-ounce glass jars that you've been saving because you are a conscientious recycler, layer the following:

miniature marshmallows	drained pineapple pieces
vanilla yogurt	drained canned sweet
chopped pecans	cherries

Clear plastic glasses may be substituted for the glass jars.

Poem

Prelutsky, Jack. "My Garden." In *Kermit's Garden of Verses*. Random House and Henson Associates, 1982.

Word Play

A terrarium is a miniature greenhouse. It is made of glass. An old saying states, "People who live in glass houses should not throw stones."

Read More About It

Carlson, Laurie. *EcoArt.* Williamson, 1993. pp. 76-77. (P-I).

Hershey, Rebecca. *Ready, Set, Grow!* Goodyear, 1995. 104 pp. (P-I).

Porter, Wes. "Designing a Terrarium Garden." In *The Garden Book.* Workman, 1989. p. 57. (I).

Sunset Editors. *Best Kids Garden Book.* Sunset, 1992. pp. 32-33. (I).

Walters, Jennie. "A Bottle Garden." *Gardening with Peter Rabbit.* Warne, 1992. pp. 44-46. (P-I).

Chapter 2
BOTANY

In order to build a conceptual framework about plant life before launching a gardening program, you may wish to do the activities in this chapter. Others of you may prefer to jump right into planning and planting the garden and do this botany unit after you have plants in your own garden to talk about.

Either way, the books and activities in this unit relate to the study of plant parts and their function, seeds, plant reproduction, and plant classification.

Some activities are best done at certain times of the year. The unit "Seeds" is best done in late Summer or early Autumn. "Reproduction" as well as "Plant Families" are best done at the height of the flowering season. You can tell that this is not one of those nicely sequenced manuals; you will have to do some juggling depending on the seasons, what is growing, and what topics you wish to cover. You're in charge.

2.1 Plant Parts

Burnie, David. *Plant*. Knopf, 1989. 64 pp. (P-I).

Botany for the grade school set. Only one of the many books in the Eyewitness Books series, this volume shows plant parts in clear, close-up photographs in the distinctive contemporary layout for which Eyewitness Books are known. The function of each plant part is explained with minimal text.

Gardening Activity

Plant Part Potted Gardens

If you are starting this activity in late Summer or early Autumn, take your boys and girls on a field trip to several local gardens to look for, identify, and discuss roots, stems, leaves, fruit, and flowers that are edible. If you are doing this activity in the Spring, have your children plant and label appropriately large terra-cotta pots, half-barrels, or plastic planters with seeds or seedlings of those plants that have been identified as having edible plant parts. For instance have a pot for roots (carrots), stems (bok choy), leaves (lettuce), flowers (nasturtiums), seeds (dill), and fruit (tomatoes). When harvesttime comes, remind your group of the plant part's function and reread the book.

Language Arts Activity

Plant Part Riddles

After reading *Plant* or one of the books in the "Read More About It" section, have the children review plant parts and their functions. Remind your group that plant parts have functions that are of use to the plant and that selected plant parts are useful to people. Distribute names of various plants to each child in your class, club, or group. Have them identify the edible parts of the plant and write a riddle that describes the plant part, its function, and its use. Other boys and girls must guess the name of the plant and its part. An example might be:

I am round and red, sometimes green.

I hold seeds and lots of food for the new plant inside my skin.

When people bite into me I make a crunchy sound.

Answer: apple; fruit.

Creative Activity

Plant Part Prints

Materials:

Parts of many plants

tempera paint

paint brushes

manilla paper

heavy books

newspapers

Read these directions to your boys and girls and proceed to do the activity:

On the newspaper arrange slices, pieces, and cross sections of plants in a design or pattern that pleases you. Repeated patterns create a pleasing effect. Some ideas include: the cross section of a small onion, an entire leaf, a flower such as a daisy, a stem, or washed-off roots. Quickly paint each piece with tempera paint. Press a sheet of manilla or construction paper on top of the painted and arranged plant parts. Weight with a heavy book for a few minutes, then remove the book and the paper carefully so the pieces are not disturbed.

Once your children get the hang of this technique, they may want to make notecards, wrapping paper, writing paper, lunch bags, and other decorated paper products.

Treat

Plant Part Stir Fry

Assemble some plant parts. For example:

zucchini—fruit   bok choy—stems
onions—roots   and leaves
fennel—seeds   carrots—roots

Chop everything into bite-size or smaller pieces. Plan to make enough for about 1/3 cup for each individual. Heat oil in a fry pan or wok. Add ingredients in this order: onions, carrots, zucchini, bok choy. Saute until tender. Sprinkle a teaspoon of fennel seeds over all. Serve.

Poem

Baldwin, Marjorie. "The Nature Lesson." In *Shades of Green*, by Anne Harvey. Greenwillow, 1991.

Word Play

When an idea, person, or group has become firmly established, we say, "It has taken root." An old folksong poses this riddle: To ope their trunks the trees are never seen. How then do they put on their robes of green? They leave them out!

Whenever we want to cheer someone on we say, "I'm going to root for you."

Read More About It

Eyewitness Visual Dictionaries. *The Visual Dictionary of Plants*. Dorling Kindersley, 1992. 64 pp. (I).

Ganeri, Anita. *Plants*. Watts, 1992. 32 pp. (P-I). Illustrated by Adrian Lascom.

Hunken, Jorie. *Botany for All Ages*. Globe Pequot, 1993. 184 pp. (I-Adult).

Mayes, Susan. *What Makes a Flower Grow?* Usborne, 1989. 24 pp. (P-I).

Royston, Angela. *What's Inside? Plants*. Dorling Kindersley, 1992. 17 pp. (P).

Watts, Claire, and Alexandra Parsons. *Make It Work! Plants*. Macmillan, 1993. 48 pp. (P-I). Photography by Jon Barnes.

2.2 Reproduction: The Reason for a Flower

Cole, Joanna. *The Magic School Bus Plants Seeds*. Scholastic, 1995. 32 pp. (P-I). Illustrated by Bruce Degan.

Miss Frizzle takes to the garden dressed in a garden-print dress. This time the school bus turns into a ladybug that travels down and around stamens, anthers, and pistils to show readers and Miss Frizzle's class pollination, seed production, and dispersal.

Gardening Activity

Observing Flowers and Their Parts

Observe a variety of plants that have easy-to-see flowers, flower parts, or seeds. Suggestions are sunflowers, sweet peas, nasturtiums, poppies, zinnias, cosmos, four-o-clocks, and rose mallows. Gourd, squash, and pumpkin flowers are good choices, also. As these flowers move through the stages of flower to seed, have the children observe, photograph, or draw the flower every few days. Have them pay close attention to the changes occuring in the carpel as the plant moves from flower to seed stage.

Have the boys and girls cut a pollinated flower in half so the seed-forming stage may be observed from the inside. Supply them with magnifying glasses or jeweler's loupes to facilitate their observations.

Ask these questions and others of your own invention to elicit observation and reflection:

What pollinated this flower? Bees? Wind? Hummingbirds? Other insects?

How could a person pollinate a flower?

How are new species of plants created?

What happens when something interferes with the process of a plant moving from flowering stage to seed stage?

How does this affect the economy when it happens to crops on a large scale (jobs, wages, prices of food at the supermarket, food supply)?

End this series of lessons with an invitation to the group to synthesize what they have learned by asking, "Tell me what you have learned about flowers."

Language Arts Activity

Videotape Life Cycles

Over the course of the growing season, have each member of your group videotape the life cycle of a flowering plant that each has grown from seed. Have each youngster write a narrative or voice over that explains what is happening at each stage. Plan to include a shot of a bee pollinating the flower if appropriate and possible. Plan to have the videotapes shown at a science fair or to an audience of friends, neighbors, family, or another class or group. You may even decide to set up a display at your local shopping mall of this and other activities that your boys and girls will do during their gardening seasons.

Creative Activity

A Visual Metaphor for Seeds

Have on hand these materials: drawing paper and crayons or colored markers.

Say to the group: "Inside each seed are the tiniest parts of the plant-to-be. We can translate this notion into a type of art project. In the middle of your paper draw any tiny free-form shape with one of your crayons, like this for example:

First time   **Second time**   **Third time**

Fig. 2.1. Sample free-form shapes.

Then with another color, go around that shape a second time following the outline of the first design. Repeat with another color, then another, and another until your paper is filled with the design. Go back and fill in the spaces any way you wish: stripes, solid colors, dots, x's, o's, or squiggly lines.

Treat

Edible Flowers

Collect and eat edible flowers, such as nasturtiums, borage, calendula, chives, mint, and pansy. The flowers of squash and zucchini may be stuffed and fried. Be absolutely certain that the flowers have not been sprayed with pesticides or fertilizers.

Poem

Fisher, Aileen. "The Seed." In *Always Wondering*. HarperCollins, 1991.

Read More About It

Burnie, David. *Plant.* Knopf, 1989. 65 pp. (P-I).

Dowden, Anne. *The Clover and the Bee.* Crowell, 1990. 96 pp. (I).

———. *From Flower to Fruit.* Ticknor & Fields, 1994. 56 pp. (I).

Gibbons, Gail. *From Seed to Plant.* Holiday House, 1991. 32 pp. (P).

Pope, Joyce. *Plant Partnerships.* Facts on File, 1990. 62 pp. (I).

Watts, Claire, and Alexandra Parsons. *Make It Work! Plants.* Macmillan, 1993. 48 pp. (P-I). Photography by Jon Barnes.

2.3 Seeds

Lauber, Patricia. *Seeds: Pop, Stick, Glide*. Crown, 1981. 57 pp. (P-I). Photographs by Jerome Wexler.

If seeds were human, they'd need passports. They love to travel. Lauber tells us how they do it. Jerome Wexler's close-up photographs show the reader seeds with burrs, jelly-covered seeds, seeds that are animal food, seeds that travel on the wind, salt shaker seeds, seeds with wings, and seeds that float on water. Wexler's photographs capture the process so readers can easily see what is going on with seed travelers.

Gardening Activity

Observing Seeds

With magnifying glasses or a jeweler's loupe, pencils, and charts in hand, have boys and girls take several walks to various spots where a variety of seeds may be found. Have them fill in the seed observation charts (see fig. 2.2 on page 22).

As an alternative, this search for seeds might be set up as a treasure hunt created specifically for your neighborhood. For example:

Find the seeds that pop beside Mr. Brown's house.

Find seeds with burrs in the vacant lot between Al's Furniture and the laundromat.

Find seeds that birds help to spread on the lawn in front of the AME Church.

After the survey of seeds in your neighborhood has been made, have the children transfer the information into a bar graph format (see fig. 2.3 on page 23).

Another activity is the two-season one described by Lauber. Select plants to be observed in Spring when they blossom and in late Summer when the seeds have formed.

Language Arts Activity

Accordion Books

Materials:

an assortment of children's poetry books and anthologies (Some of the best will have older copyrights and be found at your public library.)

two pieces of cardboard, 9" x 12" for each child

two scraps of woven, not knit, cloth material, 10" x 13" for each child

one piece of unlined paper, $8\frac{1}{2}$" x 77" for each child (butcher or mural paper)

white glue

ribbon

Have the boys and girls search poetry anthologies to find poems about seeds. Their goal is to find a poem for each type of seed travel. Children should compile these poems into accordian books by each performing the following steps:

1. Cover two pieces of cardboard, 9" x 12", with woven cloth by glueing the cloth onto the cardboard.

2. Fold the $8\frac{1}{2}$"-x-77" strip of paper back and forth like a fan to make seven sections, each $8\frac{1}{2}$" x 11".

Name _____

Plant name	Drawing of the seed	How does it travel?	Where is the plant located?

Fig. 2.2. Seed observation chart.

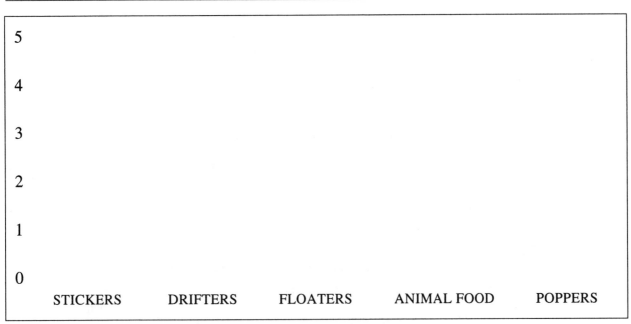

5					
4					
3					
2					
1					
0					
	STICKERS	DRIFTERS	FLOATERS	ANIMAL FOOD	POPPERS

Fig. 2.3. Sample bar graph form.

3. Glue one end to one piece of cardboard and the other end to the second piece of cardboard on the uncovered sides.

4. Attach a ribbon to the front and back covers so the book may be held closed with a bow.

5. Copy the poems onto the pages of the accordion books.

6. Decorate the book cover with designs made from seeds.

 ## Creative Activity

Seedy Photo Frames

Your boys and girls would appreciate having photographs of themselves working in their gardens or with their indoor plants. Take such photographs and then have your group construct photo frames decorated with seeds that the children have collected. Have on hand the following materials:

cardboard, 8" x 10"

a variety of seeds

white glue

clear plastic

tagboard

picture hanger

craft knife or carton cutter

Help your boys and girls cut a rectangular hole in the middle of the cardboard. This hole needs to be ¼" smaller than the photo on all sides.This cardboard is the front of the picture frame.

Have the children plan a design for the border of their picture frame.

Have them do the following:

1. With a pencil divide the frame into sections that make a pleasing design.

2. Slather the frame in small sections with white glue.

3. Section by section, attach the seeds onto the glue-covered cardboard.

4. Allow the glue to dry (read them a story while you're waiting).

5. With dabs of glue stack and attach the plastic, the photo, and the tagboard backing, in that order.

6. Attach the picture hanger.

Treat

Popcorn Balls

40 large marshmallows   1/4 cup butter
10 cups popped popcorn

Melt and blend marshmallows and butter over low heat. Pour popcorn into a large bowl. Pour marshmallow mixture over popcorn. Mix. Form into balls.

Poem

Anonymous. "Baby Seeds." In *A Child's Book of Poems,* by Gyo Fujikawa. Grosset & Dunlap, 1974.

Word Play

When people give an idea to another, they say, "I planted that seed in her head."
When a person or project has aged or has been played out, we say, "He/she/it has gone to seed."

Read More About It

Carle, Eric. *The Tiny Seed*. Picture Book Studio, 1987. 32 pp. (P).

Cole, Joanna. *The Magic School Bus Plants Seeds*. Scholastic, 1995. 32 pp. (P-I). Illustrated by Bruce Degan.

Heller, Ruth. *The Reason for a Flower*. Grosset & Dunlap, 1983. 42 pp. (P).

Jordan, Helene. *How a Seed Grows*. HarperCollins, 1992. 32 pp. (P).

Krauss, Ruth. *The Carrot Seed*. HarperCollins, 1945. (P).

Overbeck, Cynthia. *How Seeds Travel*. Lerner, 1982. 48 pp. (P-I).

Shannon, George. *Seeds*. Houghton Mifflin, 1994. 32 pp. (P). Illustrated by Steve Bjorkman.

2.4 Plants and More Plants

Rapp, Joel. *Let's Get Growing*. Prince Paperbacks, 1993. 96 pp. (I).

Joel Rapp presents indoor and outdoor gardening activities for kids that will keep them engaged and thinking. In his light conversational style he tells how to propagate plants in a variety of ways, including layering, leaf cuttings, stem cuttings, air layering, and stolon rooting. He even shows his readers how to graft a cactus. His suggestions for sharing plants with others are particularly valuable, such as his novel idea of giving them as trick-or-treat handouts at Halloween.

Gardening Activity

Plants and More Plants

Growing New Plants from Runners

Have on hand these materials:

> small glass jars, such as baby food jars, or 3" pots
>
> biodegradable containers, such as pasteboard egg cartons
>
> potting soil
>
> vermiculite
>
> watering can
>
> hairpins
>
> clean sand
>
> plants that have produced runners: strawberry or spider plants
>
> plants easily propagated by cuttings: coleus, geraniums, African violets

Help your group follow these directions:

1. Find a stolon, also called runners or daughters, of each of the larger plants.

2. Keeping the stolon attached to the parent plant, tuck the stolon into a 3" pot filled with potting soil that has been well mixed with humus and coarse sand.

3. Secure the stolon with hairpins or wire that has been bent into hairpin shapes.

4. Water.

5. Place the large plant and the potted stolon on a shelf or windowsill, being careful not to tear apart the connection.

6. Over several weeks, keep both plants moist.

7. After the stolon has firm roots and shows signs of growth, clip the connection between the larger plant and the new plant.

8. Continue to water and fertilize both plants.

Growing New Plants from Cuttings

Have your boys and girls follow these directions:

1. From a coleus or geranium plant, clip off a side shoot (stem and leaves).

2. Plant this cutting in a small pot containing a mixture of moist vermiculite and sand.

3. Place the pot in a place where it will receive light but not direct sun. Keep the soil damp. A clear plastic bag placed over the pot and plant will help keep the plant from wilting and maintain moist conditions. In a few weeks the cutting will have rooted.

Language Arts Activity

Advertising Campaign

After having raised a surplus of new plants, your boys and girls will need to have a plant sale (see "Creative Activity"). How can your group get the word out to their potential customers? Have a discussion with them centering on these questions:

Who are our potential customers? (Possible answers: neighbors, relatives, church members, library patrons, classmates.)

What are the many different ways that these people can be reached? (Posters, P.A. system ads, local TV public service announcements, newsletters, letters, fliers, word-of-mouth.)

What are our limitations, or what will keep you from being successful? (Location, money, regulations.)

How can these be overcome?

After accounting for the who, what, when, where, how, how much, how many, and why questions, develop and carry out a multimedia advertising campaign.

Creative Activity

Plant Sale

Have a plant sale by selling the newly propagated plants. Have a discussion with your group to get them thinking about how to make their sale a success. Ask questions such as:

Where shall we have our plant sale? (At a school, shopping mall, church, library, wherever there will be a lot of potential customers.)

When shall we have our plant sale? (A special day, noon, after work hours, Saturday morning, whenever there will be a lot of potential customers.)

How can we attract customers? (Decorate a sales and display area or booth; decorate the pots to make the plants more attractive; price the plants appropriately; sell food.)

How can we make a profit? (Keep costs down, sell a lot, attract lots of customers.)

What will keep our project from being successful? (Weather, regulations, attitude, lack of teamwork.)

How can these be overcome?

What will we do with the profit? (Finance the outdoor garden, start a community garden [See Chapter 11].)

After the discussion, work out a time line; assign various responsibilities; set the time, date, and place; and follow through. Advertise. Have a successful plant sale and demonstrate that money as well as plants can be propagated!

Treat

Millionaires

A successful plant sale may need some candy to sell as well. These are proven moneymakers.

1 package of caramels (14 oz.)
1 1/2 cups whole pecans
1/4 bar paraffin

3 tsp. water
8 plain chocolate bars

Melt caramels with water. Stir in pecans. Drop by the teaspoonful onto greased wax paper. Refrigerate. Melt chocolate bars and paraffin in double boiler. Dip caramel nut candies into chocolate. Place onto the wax paper. Allow to harden. Optional, place in paper candy cups.

Poem

Field, Rachel. "Taking Root." In *Taxis and Toadstools*. Doubleday, Doran, 1945.

Word Play

When a new idea, fad, or procedure catches on we say it has taken root.

Read More About It

Dietl, Ulla. *The Plant and Grow Project Book*. Sterling, 1993. 48 pp. (I).

Hershey, Rebecca. *Ready. Set. Grow*. Goodyear, 1995. 104 pp. (P-I).

Markmann, Erika. *Grow It! An Indoor/Outdoor Gardening Guide for Kids*. Random House, 1991. 47 pp. (I).

Wilkes, Angela. *My First Garden Book*. Knopf, 1992. 48 pp. (P-I).

Woolfit, Gabrielle. *Sow and Grow*. Thompson Learning, 1994. 32 pp. (P-I).

2.5 Plant Families

Lerner, Carol. *Plant Families*. Morrow Jr. Books, 1989. 32 pp. (I).

Twelve of the largest plant families are introduced to young readers. Lerner sorts out the *Compositae* from the *Umbelliferai;* the *Rosaceae* from the *Labiatae*. Each plant has particular characteristics that botanists use to place it in one category but not another. Lerner tells how this identification is done. Before this book is introduced to readers, it is recommended that they have read a more basic botany book such as *What's Inside? Plants* so that they have the background to identify plant parts.

Lerner's lovely and colorful illustrations, detailed and accurate, provide the reader with aesthetic botany lessons.

Gardening Activity

Plant Classification

How do botanists classify plants? By studying them very closely with magnification aids such as magnifying glasses and by differentiating among the various plant parts. Supply your boys and girls with as many magnifying glasses and jeweler's loupes as can be obtained. Distribute copies of the plant classification chart (fig. 2.4 on page 29). Take your group on a walk to a nearby garden or park where you have previously marked plants that you want them to identify. Have children fill in the chart and identify the plant families.

Language Arts Activity

Plant Family Riddles

Have your boys and girls write riddles about each of the plant families. Here is one example:

I have spokes and ribs.
Like an umbrella, I spread out.
Each of my teeny flowers has five petals.
What's my family name?
Answer: *Umbelliferae*

Creative Activity

Family Portraits

Help your boys and girls follow these instructions: Press and dry five different blossoms belonging to the same family. For example, use daisy, chicory, dandelion, zinnia, and gumweed, from the Composite family. This may take several weeks because these plants won't bloom simultaneously.

Materials: blotter paper or paper towels and thick, heavy books such as a big city telephone book, a dictionary, or bricks.

Flat-faced flowers: Place the flowers face down and flat on the blotter paper and press the center of the flower even flatter with your index finger.

Thick-centered flower such as daisies or zinnias: Pull the petals from the center and dry separately because the thick center takes longer.

Complex-shaped flowers (those with petals growing in several directions; for example, snapdragons or daffodils): Turn these sideways on the blotter paper when pressing.

Cluster flowers (those with florets; for example, geraniums): Pull off the florets and dry separately.

Name _____

Name of plant	Family	Leaf (look for shape arrangement on stem)	Stem (look for shape)	Blossom

Fig. 2.4. Plant classification chart.

From *Beyond the Bean Seed*. © 1996. Nancy Allen Jurenka and Rosanne J. Blass. Teacher Ideas Press. (800) 237-6124.

Spike-shaped flowers, such as larkspur and forget-me-not: Lay these on their sides on the blotter paper or paper towel.

After all the flowers have been arranged on a blotter, cover them with another piece of blotter paper or paper towel. Place between the pages of a book. Weight. Wait for two to three weeks depending on the humidity.

Using glue, mount the dried blossoms on tagboard, arranging them at various heights as might be seen in a family portrait. Fill in the remainder of the plant stems and leaves with crayon. Or be fanciful and draw dressed-up human figures underneath the flower heads.

Title the picture appropriately: The _____ Family.

Treat

Treasure Hunt Treats

Using the items in the following list, hide as many of each item as you have children in your group.

a peach   a cup of iced mint tea
some carrot sticks   a few peanuts

Supply each of your students with a paper plate and a copy of the following instructions:

Find one member each of these plant families:

Rosaceae   Labiatae
Umbelliferae   Leguminosae

When all items have been found, accounted for, and possibly redistributed so that each child has all four treats, have a family feast.

Poem

Arkell, Reginald. "Those Latin Names." In *Shades of Green,* by Anne Harvey. Greenwillow, 1991.

Word Play

Many flower names originated from Greek or Latin; these names are often descriptive of the flower. Columbine, for instance, comes from the Latin word *columba,* meaning dove. Originally, chrysanthemum comes from Greek but has been Latinized over the years. Its origins are *anth*, meaning flower, and *khrusos*, meaning gold.

Read More About It

Burnie, David. *Plant.* Knopf, 1989. 64 pp. (P-I).

Dowden, Anne Ophelia. *The Blossom on the Bough.* Crowell, 1994. 71 pp. (I).

Eyewitness Visual Directories. *The Visual Dictionary of Plants.* Dorling Kindersley, 1992. 64 pp. (I).

Fenton, Carroll, and Herminie Kitchen. *Plants We Live On.* John Day, 1971. 128 pp. (I).

Hausherr, Rosmarie. *What Food Is This?* Scholastic, 1994. 40 pp. (P).

Hunken, Jorie. *Botany for All Ages.* Globe Pequot, 1993. 184 pp. (I-Adult).

Chapter 3
FLOWERS

In this set of lessons children are introduced to a variety of flowers, including flowers for fun such as the sunflower and morning glory.

No attempt at scientific classification is made here. The decision about what flowers to include was based upon what books were available and what categories these books seemed to form.

Most lessons will need to be accomplished in the major growing season for your locality. The bulb lesson could be done in the Autumn or early Winter.

3.1 Flowers

Lobel, Arnold. *The Rose in My Garden.* Morrow, 1993. 40 pp. (P-I). Illustrated by Anita Lobel.

Using the cumulative tale style of traditional folk literature, the story begins with a bee that falls asleep on a rose; the narrator then adds flower after flower. Eventually, a cat comes along to bring the tale to a close with a surprise ending. Anita Lobel's lush floral illustrations make this droll tale a treasure. Youth leaders and teachers seeking ways to increase children's ability to play with language will appreciate the repeated storyline.

Gardening Activity

Select Flowers to Plant

Select flowers to plant from the Lobels' book. Some are annuals, some are perennials, and still others are biennials. Some are bulbs and some are shrubs. What you choose to plant will depend on your planting site, geographic location, and time of year. Marigolds, zinnias, tulips, and amaryllis are likely to be successful choices in any setting. Let the selection process lead you to investigate different kinds of flowering plants.

Language Arts Activity

Retell Using Puppets

Retell the tale by acting it out using stick puppets. Assign a specific flower to each child. Remember to include the bee, the cat, and the fieldmouse. Children may wish to select a narrator to retell the tale while they act it out, or they may prefer to each recite the text that presents their flowers.

Creative Activity

Make Stick Puppets

Make stick puppets. Draw or cut pictures from garden catalogs. Cut Styrofoam meat trays into sticks. Staple pictures onto Styrofoam sticks.

Treat

Iced Honey Sip

Place 1 quart of water and 2/3 cup honey in a jar with a lid. Shake well, chill, and serve iced.

Poem

Holland, Rupert Sargeant. "Foolish Flowers." In *Favorite Poems for Children*, ed. Holly Pell McConnougly. Barnes & Noble, 1993.

Word Play

Flower names sometimes reflect the flower's resemblance to something else, such as the names foxgloves, bachelor buttons, or lady's slippers. "Foolish Flowers" plays with flower names such as these.

Read More About It

Burnie, David. *Flowers.* Dorling Kindersley, 1992. 61 pp. (P-I).

Cousins, Lucy. *Flower in the Garden.* Candlewick Press, 1992. 8 pp. (P).

Eaton, Marge. *Flower Pressing.* Lerner, 1973. 32 pp. (P-I).

Laird, Elizabeth. *Rosy's Garden: A Child's Keepsake of Flowers.* Philomel, 1990. 46 pp. (P-I). Illustrated by Satomi Ichikawa.

Marsh, Janet. *A Child's Book of Flowers.* Hutchinson, 1993. 59 pp. (I).

Richardson, Joy. *Flowers.* Franklin Watts, 1993. 29 pp. (P).

3.2 Tulips, Daffodils, and Other Bulbs

Robbins, Ken. *A Flower Grows*. Dial, 1988. 32 pp. (P-I).

This picture book shows the growth of an amaryllis. A series of paintings shows the bud about to bloom, its unfolding, and then the fading of the flower. Replenishment of the bulb's food supply by the remaining green leaves is explained. Instructions with illustrations for planting and raising the bulb are given. After sharing the story, plan to grow your own amaryllis. This rapidly growing flower provides a dramatic introduction to bulbs.

Gardening Activity

Forcing Bulbs

Select and plant a variety of bulbs for indoor forcing. In addition to the tropical amaryllis, include cool-climate bulbs that require Winter-like chilling, such as tulips or daffodils, and that do not require chilling, such as paperwhite narcissus.

Language Arts Activity

Bulb Family Tree

Identify members of the bulb family (bulbs, corms, tubers, and rhizomes) and create a family tree of bulb varieties. Be sure to include common foods such as potatoes, onions, and garlic. Describe the characteristics of each variety.

Discover the differences between varieties by dissecting and examining bulbs from each family. Examine at least two bulbs from each family so that you can slice one bulb vertically and the other horizontally to observe and compare their structure. Discuss and then draw pictures of bulb varieties. Display the drawings with the family tree.

Creative Activity

Bulb Prints

Using dissected bulbs and tempera paints, create bulb prints. Display the prints with the family tree and drawings.

Treat

Saffron Cookies

Saffron, the world's rarest and most expensive spice, is obtained from the dried stigmas of *Crocus sativus* blossoms.

1 cup butter	2 1/2 cups flour
3/4 cup sugar	1/2 tsp. baking powder
1 egg	1/8 tsp. salt

1/4 tsp. ground saffron soaked in 1 Tbsp. hot water

Cream the butter and sugar. Beat in the egg, then the saffron and water. Gradually sift in the flour, baking powder, and salt. Refrigerate until firm. Shape into balls. Place on baking sheet. Flatten into round cookies with the back of a fork. Bake at 400° for 7 to 10 minutes.

Poem

Fisher, Aileen. "The Daffodils." In *Cricket in a Thicket*. Scribner's, 1963.

Word Play

"To gild the lily" is a phrase used when someone applies excessive decoration or ornamentation to an item that is already beautiful or valuable.

Read More About It

Crowell, Robert. *The Lore and Legend of Flowers*. Putnam, 1982. pp. 4-26. (I). Illustrated by Anne Ophelia Dowden.

Krasilovsky, Phyllis. *The First Tulips in Holland*. Doubleday, 1982. 32 pp. (P-I).

Laird, Elizabeth. *Rosy's Garden: A Child's Keepsake of Flowers*. Philomel, 1990. pp. 12-13. (P-I). Illustrated by Satomi Ichikawa.

O'Callahan, Jay. *Tulips*. Picture Book Studio, 1992. 26 pp. (P). Illustrated by Debrah Santini.

Pohl, Kathleen. *Tulips*. Steck-Vaughn, 1986. 32 pp. (P-I).

Selsam, Millicent. *Bulbs, Corms, and Such*. Morrow, 1974. 48 pp. (P-I). Photographs by Jerome Wexler.

3.3 Fun Flowers

Johnson, Sylvia. *Morning Glory*. Lerner, 1985. 48 pp. (I). Photographs by Yuko Sato.

The development of the morning glory, from the planting of the seed to the dying of the withered vines and dispersal of new seeds, is presented in extensive detail. Colored photos include labelled cross sections of the plant and seed. Of particular interest are a series of photos of the blossom that follow as it begins to open at 3:00 AM and is fully open by 4:00 AM. The book concludes with a one-page discussion of the morning glory family, which includes bindweed, dodder, and the vining sweet potato, and a glossary of technical terms.

Gardening Activity

Flower Clock Garden

Morning glories, sunflowers, and dandelions can be used to tell time. Design and plant a flower clock garden using these and other flowers, such as four-o'clocks, that will tell time.

Language Arts Activity

Flower Clock Garden Signs

Have on hand the following materials:

Balsa wood cut into 9"-x-13" pieces

wooden stakes

8½"-x-11" paper

seed catalogs

colored markers

scissors

glue

¾" tacks

tack hammer

polyurethane varnish

Read these directions to your boys and girls:

Design a garden sign to identify the flowers in your clock garden. Draw a picture of the flower on the paper or cut one out of the seed catalog and glue it onto the paper. Label the flower and tell something about it, such as the time it tells and how it tells time. Glue the paper to the balsa wood to which a stake has been attached. In a well-ventilated area apply the polyurethane varnish over the paper so it is protected from weather. Be certain to follow the directions on the varnish container. Place the sign in an appropriate place in the flower clock garden.

Creative Activity

Dandelion Spinners

Cut dandelion stems 4" long.

Make three slits in one end of stem.

Use a pencil to roll the stem ends as if making curls.

Slide a toothpick through the hollow stem.

Blow on your spinner or let the wind turn it.

Treat

Dandelion Leaves
with Sunflower Seeds

Serve dandelion leaves in a green salad or cook and serve like spinach. Sprinkle the salad or cooked leaves with sunflower seeds.

Poem

Farjeon, Eleanor. "Morning Glory." In *Eleanor Farjeon's Poems for Children*. Lippincott, 1984. (I).

Read More About It

Ford, Miela. *Sunflower*. Greenwillow, 1995. 26 pp. (P).

Goldenberg, Janet. *Wierd Things You Can Grow*. Random House, 1994. 48 pp. (P-I). Illustrated by Phoebe Gloeckner.

King, Elizabeth. *Backyard Sunflower*. Dutton, 1993. 32 pp. (P).

Lovejoy, Sharon. *Sunflower Houses: Garden Discoveries for Children of All Ages*. Interweave, 1995. 144 pp. (I).

Lovejoy, Sharon. *Hollyhock Houses*. Interweave, 1994. 95 pp. (I).

Overbeck, Cynthia. *Sunflower*. Lerner, 1981. 48 pp. (I).

Selsam, Millicent, and Jerome Wexler. *The Amazing Dandelion*. Morrow, 1977. 46 pp. (P-I).

———. *Mimosa: The Sensitive Plant*. Morrow, 1978. 48 pp. (P).

3.4 Flowering Alphabets

Lobel, Anita. *Alison's Zinnia*. Greenwillow, 1990. 32 pp. (P).

Richly colored floral art by Anita Lobel captures our eye as linked sentences take us through the book. A gift to both teachers and gardeners, the story line sets up an opportunity for sentence pattern practice: name—verb—flower. Lessons that link writing to reading are easily accomplished using this book. Worth noting is the author-illustrator's explanation about how the book came to be.

Gardening Activity

Alphabet Garden

Plant a flowering alphabet garden. Let children select and plant flowers that correspond to the letters of their own names. Fill in missing letters with the names of family members.

Language Arts Activity

Alphabet Book

Write and illustrate your own flowering alphabet book. Use the names of children and their family members with the corresponding flowers that you planted.

Creative Activity

Potpourri

　　　　1 quart dried petals and leaves

　　　　3 tablespoons orris root or other fixative

　　　　½ cup dried herbs

　　　　2 teaspoons of an essential oil that you like such as orange, lemon, jasmine, or rose (available from drug or craft stores)

　　　　2-3 tablespoons spices

Follow these directions:

1. Mix fixative and oil. Cover. Store 48 hours. Shake often.

2. Mix dried herbs and flowers.

3. Add spices, fixative, and oil mixture.

4. Cover. Store three to four weeks. Stir and shake every few days.

5. Place in a pretty bowl or use to make sachets.

Treat

Nasturtium Salad

green nasturtium seeds   1 head lettuce
chopped nasturtium flowers   French dressing

Add nasturtium leaves to lettuce. Add seeds to dressing.
Toss together. Decorate with flowers.

Poem

Rands, William Brighty. "The Lavender Bed." In *Favorite Poems for Children*, ed. Holly Pell McConnaugly. Barnes & Noble, 1993. p. 34.

Word Play

"Red as a rose" is a common simile in which the adjective starts with the same letter as the plant.

Read More About It

Christensen, Bonnie. *An Edible Alphabet Book*. Dial, 1994. 32 pp. (P).

Pallotta, Jerry. *The Flower Alphabet Book*. Charlesbridge, 1988. 32 pp. (P). Illustrated by Leslie Evans.

Tillett, Leslie. *Plant and Animal Alphabet Coloring Book*. Dover, 1980. 48 pp. (P-I).

Wilner, Isabel. *A Garden Alphabet*. Dutton, 1991. 32 pp. (P).

Yolen, Jane. *Elfabet: An ABC of Elves*. Little, Brown, 1990. 32 pp. (P).

3.5 Wildflowers

Beame, Rona. *Wildflowers: A Collector's Album.* Random House, 1994. 56 pp. (I). Illustrated by Dianne McElwain.

After opening this book tied shut with a pretty ribbon, boys and girls are treated to watercolor paintings of wildflowers sorted by classes and the directions for collecting, pressing, and air drying them. Directions for mounting wildflowers within the book itself are given. Important to catch is the "Wildflower Collector's Code." In the book the address for the National Wildflower Research Center is out-of-date. Since the book has been published, the address has been changed to 4801 LaCrosse Blvd., Austin, TX 78739. The last section gives the instructions for several craft projects that may be done with the wildflowers that the children have collected. Beame and McElwain have created a beautiful book that children are likely to save for a lifetime once they have filled it with wildflowers.

Gardening Activity

Pick, Press, and Plant

Gather wildflowers and wildflower seeds. Be sure to select a gathering site where wildflowers are growing in abundance. Pick only a few in any one site leaving enough for the next person to pick and enough to continue growing. Press the wildflowers. Plant the seeds. Sow the seeds in neglected corners, vacant lots, sidewalk cracks, or along parking lot fences. Encourage discussion of the difference between wildflowers and weeds. If you wish to create a wildflower garden, contact your local Cooperative Extension office, soil conservation service, nursery or garden center for help with selecting your site and plants.

Language Arts Activity

Wildflower Game Book

Discuss with your children wildflower games that they may know. Weaving clover chains, plucking daisy petals while reciting "loves me, loves me not," or twirling a buttercup under the chin to see "who likes butter" are likely to be familiar games. Follow up by interviewing family members, friends, and neighbors to learn about additional wildflower games. Compile your own book of wildflower games. Sharon Lovejoy's *Sunflower Houses* and Jeanne Chesanow's *Honeysuckle Sipping: The Plant Lore of Childhood* are excellent sources of flower games and toys.

Creative Activity

Press Wildflowers

Place flowers between two pieces of newspaper. Put the newspaper under a stack of heavy books or between the pages of a telephone directory. Set one or two heavy books on top of the telephone directory. Let sit for one to four weeks until dry and flat. The length of time needed will depend on the humidity of your climate.

Use your pressed wildflowers to make bookmarks. Position flowers on tagboard or light-weight cardboard. Cover by laminating or using clear contact paper.

Treat

Root Beer

Serve root beer.

Find out about and try some edible wild plants. *Plantworks* by Karen Shanberg and Stan Tekula is a wild plant cookbook, field guide, and activity book for the novice and naturalist. *Dandelions* by Eiicki Asayama tells how to make soup or salad from dandelions.

Poem

Rockwell, Anne. "Me and My Weeds." In *The Big Book for Our Planet,* ed. Ann Durell, Jean Craighead George, and Katherine Paterson. Dutton, 1993.

Word Play

Two two-syllable words that sound alike except for the initial sound are called a hinky pinky. Two one- and three-syllable words are called hink pink and hinkety pinkety. Some examples of wildflower hinky pinkies are flower power, crazy daisy, and thistle missile.

Read More About It

Busch, Phyllis. *Wildflowers and the Stories Behind Their Names.* Scribner's, 1977. 88 pp. (I). Illustrated by Anne Ophelia Dowden.

Lerner, Carol. *Flowers of a Woodland Spring.* Morrow, 1979. 28 pp. (I).

McMillan, Bruce. *Counting Wildflowers.* Lothrop, Lee & Shepard, 1986. 32 pp. (P).

Samson, Suzanne. *Fairy Dusters and Blazing Stars: Exploring Wildflowers.* Roberts Rinehart, 1994. 32 pp. (P-I).

Velghe, Anne. *Wildflowers: A Primer.* Farrar, Straus & Giroux, 1994. 32 pp. (P-I).

Wexler, Jerome. *Jack-in-the-Pulpit.* Dutton, 1993. 38 pp. (P-I).

————. *Queen Anne's Lace.* Whitman, 1994. 32 pp. (P-I).

Chapter 4
VEGETABLES

Vegetable books for children number in the dozens. One might be lead to believe that vegetables are a child's favorite food! Perhaps overcooked frozen broccoli served on a Winter's night may cause whines but that scene is countered by the whoops of a proud child pulling up her first carrot.

Vegetable cultivation is a significant part of many children's garden programs. This unit supports that trend by focusing on specific vegetables.

Most activities are designed with the assumption that you have access to a children's garden, even if it means a collection of large containers. Most of the featured vegetables can be grown in containers, pumpkins being the exception. However, if your group succeeds in growing pumpkins in a container, we would love to hear about it.

This unit is best done during the major growing season in your part of the country. However, you decide when you want to do the various activities. Tomatoes can even be grown in Winter if you grow them hydroponically. This unit is not designed to be followed in any rigid sequence, so read through the entire unit, then decide when you wish to do what. Your circumstances will dictate the decision.

4.1 Vegetables

Ehlert, Lois. *Growing Vegetable Soup*. Harcourt Brace Jovanovich, 1987. 32 pp. (P).
Visually exciting, this picture book gives a simplified step-by-step process for growing 11 vegetables. A vegetable soup recipe is provided.

Gardening Activity

Growing Vegetable Soup

Grow some or all of the vegetables: green beans, green peas, corn, zucchini, carrot, tomato, potato, broccoli, onions, peppers, and cabbage. To speed things up you may want to use Burpee Sure Starts® for the tomatoes and peppers. Also, you may want to try early producing, patio, or miniature varieties.

Language Arts Activity

Vegies A to Z

Read Jerry Pallota's *The Flower Alphabet Book* to your group. Using that book as a model, in which Jerry Pallotta has written anecdotes about Leslie Evans's illustrations, have your boys and girls create a *Vegetable Alphabet Book*. The children will need to do research about the vegetables they have chosen to find interesting information they could use to write their anecdotes.

The vegetable pictures could be cut out of construction paper, drawn, and crayoned, or clipped from seed catalogs. For the letter "X" try "xeriscape" and use drought-resistant vegetables. Read Pallota's *Alphabet Vegetable* to the group after their books are made.

This writing activity could be be transformed into a speaking activity. The children could dress in colors appropriate for their vegetable and read in turn their vegetable captions to an audience.

Creative Activity

Vegetable Seed Markers

Gather the following materials:

     a variety of brightly colored glossy papers

     dark blue, dark brown, black, or white poster board precut into 4"-x-6" cards

     scissors

     glue

     popsicle sticks

Help your girls and boys follow these directions: Cut out vegetable shapes from brilliantly colored papers. Glue them onto the dark, white, or black poster board. Call the attention of your group members to the contrasts in color. Attach the vegetable signs to popsicle sticks. Have the children place these in the garden in the appropriate places where they have planted vegetable seeds or plants.

Treat

One Gallon Vegetable Soup

2 quarts beef broth	1 cup lima beans
2 quarts tomato juice	1 cup green beans
1 onion, diced	1 cup green peas
2 stalks celery, diced	1 cup cabbage, chopped
1 cup carrots, diced	2 potatoes, diced
1 cup corn	1/4 cup parsley, chopped
1 Tbs. fresh basil, chopped	salt and pepper

Place everything except the potatoes and the seasonings in a kettle and simmer for 20 minutes. Add potatoes and cook for 30 minutes. Add the basil and parsley. Simmer for 5 minutes. Season to taste.

Poem

Field, Rachel. "Vegetables." In *V Is for Verses*, by Odille Ousley. Ginn, 1964.

Word Play

When something is worthless, we say, "It isn't worth a hill of beans."

When a person is being admired because she is an expert on a subject, we say, "Wow, she sure knows her onions."

Read More About It

Florian, Douglas. *Vegetable Garden*. Harcourt Brace Jovanovich, 1991. 32 pp. (P).

Hitte, Kathryn, and William Hayes. *Mexicali Soup*. Parents Magazine Press, 1970. 38 pp. (P-I).

Sobol, Harriet. *A Book of Vegetables*. Dodd, Mead, 1984. 46 pp. (P-I).

Thomas, Elizabeth. *Green Beans*. Carolrhoda, 1992. (P).

Waters, Marjorie. *The Victory Garden Kids' Book*. Globe Pequot, 1994. 148 pp. (I).

4.2 Pumpkins

McDonald, Megan. *The Great Pumpkin Switch*. Orchard, 1992. 32 pp. (P-I). Illustrated by Ted Lewin.

In this picture book illustrated by Ted Lewin, Grandpa tells a story from his childhood in which his friend Otto and he accidently saw off his sister Rosie's special Big Max pumpkin from the vine. It crashes down the stairs and breaks into pieces. They know that they are in deep trouble. Fortunately, they recover by purchasing a replacement pumpkin from Mr. Angelo and all turns out well.

Garden Activity

Create a Pumpkin Patch

Depending on your circumstances, grow many pumpkins, a few pumpkins, gigantic pumpkins, tiny pumpkins, just the right size pumpkins, or white pumpkins. Or take a trip to someone's pumpkin patch in the late Autumn to enjoy and observe pumpkins.

If you have your own pumpkin patch or have access to one in the early Summer, have your boys and girls try one of the following activities:

Slip a newly forming pumpkin into an odd-shaped plastic bottle or jar or a commercially available vegetable mold.

Scratch a name or message into a pumpkin shell in early Summer.

Your group will enjoy seeing the results of these early interventions when they harvest their pumpkins in the Autumn.

Language Arts Activity

Write a Fable

A fable is a very brief didactic tale in which nonhuman characters learn a lesson in life that could apply to human lives. Read *Aesop's Fables*, Lobel's *Fables*, or Demi's *Reflective Fables* to your group so that they get a notion of just what a fable is all about.

Start the writing part of the lesson by listing a few morals and truisms on a chart or chalkboard, such as the following:

A penny saved is a penny earned.

A fool and his money are soon parted.

Look before you leap.

Necessity is the mother of invention.

If at first you don't succeed, try, try, again.

After these have been listed, ask your boys and girls to pick one of these morals or one of their own and then write a fable that features a pumpkin or a pumpkin vine come to life as one of the main characters.

Creative Activity

Pumpkin as an Art Form

Naturally children will want to make jack-o'-lanterns, and, with the carving tools now on the market, jack-o'-lantern carving has been taken to new creative heights.

What other uses for an art project might a pumpkin have? Brainstorm with your boys and girls. What could be created if pumpkins were:

carved in designs other than faces,
strung together,
turned upside down,
stacked,
turned into containers (for what?), or turned into a painted sculpture?

Pick one, or more, and do it. Play around with being creative. Read aloud Cavaragno's book, *Pumpkin People*, to see what creative uses these people made of pumpkins.

Treat

Pumpkin Cupcakes

1 cup pumpkin puree	1 1/4 cups flour
1 stick margarine	1/2 teaspoon baking powder
3/4 sugar	1/2 teaspoon baking soda
2 eggs	1 teaspoon pumpkin pie spice
1/3 cup water	

Cream margarine and sugar. Add eggs. Beat. Add pumpkin and water. Beat. Sift dry ingredients into the mixture. Stir until incorporated. Pour the batter into muffin tins lined with paper cupcake liners. Bake for 20 to 25 minutes at 350°.

Yield: 12 cupcakes.

Poem

Sandburg, Carl. "Theme in Yellow." In *Go with the Poem*, by Lilian Moore. McGraw-Hill, 1979.

Word Play

Parents will sometimes refer fondly to their children as "Punkin" or "Little Pumpkin."

Read More About It

Cavagnaro, David, and Maggie Cavagnaro. *The Pumpkin People*. Sierra Club Books, 1979. 32 pp. (P-I).

Gillis, Jennifer. *In a Pumpkin Shell*. Storey Communications, 1992. 58 pp. (P-I).

Johnson, Hannah. *From Seed to Jack O'Lantern*. Lothrop, Lee & Shepard, 1974. 42 pp. (P-I).

King, Elizabeth. *The Pumpkin Patch*. Dutton, 1990. 38 pp. (P).

Zagwyn, Deborah. *The Pumpkin Blanket*. Celestial Arts, 1990. 32 pp. (P).

4.3 Tomatoes

Watts, Barrie. *Tomato*. Silver Burdett, 1990. 24 pp. (P).

Vivid color photography brings the reader into close-up contact with tomato plants, flowers, fruit, and seeds. The tomato life cycle is shown in step-by-step photographic sequence throughout the book. From seed to harvest, close-up photographs and drawings explain to the young reader how a tomato grows. The author wants his book read by several ages. He puts important information in boldface print and simple language for the beginning reader and provides more detailed descriptions for the second-grade reader.

Gardening Activity

Hydroponics

Tomato culture provides your group an opportunity to experiment with hydroponics. Collect these materials:

> tomato seedlings
>
> a large plastic food storage box with snug-fitting lid
>
> plant food
>
> water
>
> knife
>
> aquarium pump and an air breaker (these last two may be obtained from a pet store)

Provide these directions to your group:

1. Dilute plant food in water. Fill the plastic container with the water up to two inches from the top. Place the aquarium pump and the air breaker into the container.

2. Cut a hole large enough to accommodate the cord of the pump at the edge of the lid of the container. Cut holes in the lid about 5" apart for the tomato seedlings. Wiggle the cord through the hole and place the lid onto the container.

3. Push the tomato seedlings (with cleaned-off roots) through the holes in the lid.

4. Stuff paper towels around the holes for the seedlings and the cord.

5. Place the whole apparatus in a sunny spot or under a plant light. Plug in the pump.

6. As the tomato plants grow, they will need to be supported with string or some other brace.

7. Every two weeks add diluted plant food to the water and keep the water level up.

Language Arts Activity

Five Senses-Based Creative Writing

Use a five senses chart with your boys and girls as a way to kick off a story about Tommie Tomato, an imaginary tomato puppet with magical powers. Before the writing begins, divide a huge piece of paper—say, 36" x 52"—or a chalkboard into five columns. Label the columns with the following headings: "Feels," "Smells," "Looks," "Sounds," and "Tastes."

Distribute luscious, vine-ripened tomatoes to your group. Have them observe their tomatoes. Elicit from the group words that would fit into each sense category, except the taste category. Then have them eat their tomatoes and suggest "tasting" words.

Distribute tomato-shaped, lined writing paper and pens, and ask your boys and girls to write an anecdote or story about the imaginary adventures of Tommie Tomato. Be sure to remind them that they may add to and use the words in the chart. Remind them that spelling doesn't count. Tell them they may scribble spell troublesome words. Staple their stories to tomato-shaped red construction paper covers.

Creative Activity

Tommie Tomato Puppet

Have your kids make a tomato puppet using the puppet pattern (fig. 4.1 on page 51) provided with this lesson. Use red-orange polished cotton or felt for the main body and head. Use felt scraps for facial features. Fashion a leafy collar from green felt or polished cotton. Enlarge the pattern if necessary.

Treat

Tommie Tomato Cake

2 cups sugar
2 Tbs. shortening
4 beaten eggs
2 cups canned tomato soup
4 cups flour

2 tsp. baking soda
1 tsp. cinnamon
1/2 tsp. nutmeg
1/2 tsp. cloves
2 cups raisins

Combine ingredients in the order as written. Mix well with each addition. If the batter is too thick, add water, a tablespoon at a time. Pour into two 6-cup bundt pans and one ovenproof glass custard cup. Bake the bundt cakes at 250° for one hour. Bake the custard cup for 20 minutes. Cool on rack.

Assemble. With flat sides frosted together, stack and frost the bundt cakes with red-colored frosting.

Frosting (Note: Before adding the red coloring, remove 1/4 cup of frosting.):
1/2 cup butter
1 lb. confectioners sugar
1 tsp. grated lemon rind
2 fresh egg yolks

1 Tbs. milk
small bottle red food coloring
few drops green food coloring

Cream butter. Add sugar. Beat in egg yolks, lemon rind, and milk. Add the small bottle of red food coloring. Mix well. Spread over the cake.

Stem: Color the remaining frosting with green food coloring. Set the cupcake atop the assembled and frosted bundt cakes. Frost the cupcake with green frosting. Add candy leaves if desired.

Decorations: Fashion facial features (a big smile) from licorice and oversized sunglasses from round jelly fruit slices and licorice.

Poem

Livingston, Myra Cohn. "Tomato Time." In *Shoots of Green: Poems for Young Gardeners,* by Ella Bramblett. Crowell, 1968.

 **Word Play**

In the 1940s a pretty woman was referred to as a "tomato."

Read More About It

Fell, Derek. *A Kid's First Book of Gardening*. Running Press, 1989. pp. 53-55. (P-I).

Johnson, Stephanie. *Tomatoes and Other Killer Vegetable Jokes*. Doherty, 1992. 128 pp. (P-I).

Selsam, Millicent. *The Tomato and Other Fruit Vegetables*. Morrow, 1970. 47 pp. (P).

Sobol, Harriet. *A Book of Vegetables*. Dodd, Mead, 1984. 45 pp. (P-I).

Walters, Jennie. "Window-sill Tomatoes." In *Gardening with Peter Rabbit*. Warne, 1992. pp. 16-17. (P-I).

Waters, Marjorie. *The Victory Garden Kids' Book*. Globe Pequot, 1994. pp. 134-135. (I).

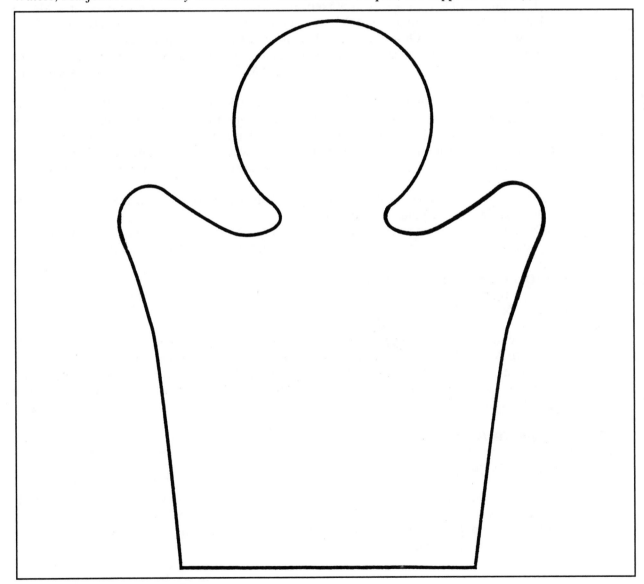

Fig. 4.1. Tommie Tomato Pattern.

From *Beyond the Bean Seed*. © 1996. Nancy Allen Jurenka and Rosanne J. Blass. Teacher Ideas Press. (800) 237-6124.

4.4 Potatoes

Meltzer, Milton. *The Amazing Potato*. HarperCollins, 1992. 116 pp. (I).

Award-winning history writer Milton Meltzer focuses his talent on the potato, a lowly vegetable to which millions in the world owe their existence. Is that a grandiose claim? After reading this book that tells of the potato's origins, history, cultivation requirements, and economic significance, children are likely to be impressed with this $100-billion-a-year vegetable.

Gardening Activity

Grow Potatoes

Take your children to the local nursery or invite a local nursery employee or a Master Gardener to talk to your group about the varieties of potato that do well in your area. Have your group ask questions about how they should plant and care for their potatoes.

When you select your potatoes for planting make certain that they are certified disease-free seed potatoes. You may wish to try the varieties that Meltzer mentions in his books such as the Red Pontiac.

Potatoes need to be planted in 4-inch holes that are 18 inches apart. Have the children find the eyes of the potato. Then have them cut the potatoes into four parts, making certain that there are two eyes in each section. Plant the potatoes so that the eyes are facing up. Cover the sections with soil that has been mixed with compost. In a few weeks the potato plants will be growing and will have produced flowers. At this stage the youngsters may dig gently for new potatoes— a tiny delectable treat!

Now it's time to mound the dirt 3 to 4 inches. This will make room for the potatoes to grow to maturity. Harvest the potatoes in late Summer.

Caution: Potatoes do produce fruit after flowering. The fruit is poisonous. Don't eat the fruit and make certain your youngsters know the difference between a fruit and a tuber.

Language Arts Activity

Potato News

Create newspapers devoted to each chapter of Meltzer's book. What kinds of articles would the *Potato News* contain? What headlines? What articles would appear in the society section, sports, home arts, comics, crossword puzzle, letters to the editor, advice column, and poetry column for each period of potato history? Have fun as well as have the children dig into a slice of potato history.

Creative Activity

Potato Frogs

Several creative activities could be done with potatoes, including creating Mr. Potato Heads or making potato prints. Directions for making potato prints may be found in *Sunset Best Kids' Garden Book,* pages 48-49. However, using a potato as a frog for arranging flowers has interesting aesthetic possibilities.

Create potato frog flower arrangements, an idea from the artist Bruno Munari in his children's nonfiction book, *A Flower with Love*. Have on hand the following materials:

potatoes

knitting needle

shallow containers

flowers

water

knife

foliage

bare branches

Read these directions to your group:

Slice a potato in half lengthwise or crosswise. Jab holes all over the rounded part with a knitting needle. Place the potato flat side down in a shallow china, pottery, or glass container. Next, insert branches in the holes to give structure or shape to the arrangement. These shapes could suggest a fan, a right angle, or a "half of a basketball" shape. Then add the main flowers, remembering to place the darker and more dense shapes near the bottom of the arrangement and the lighter, more feathery or dainty flowers near the top. Fill in with leaves and the rest of the flowers, taking care to maintain the design outlined by the branches.

Give your arrangement to someone who could use an expression of your good feelings or appreciation.

Treat

Mashed Potato Candy

Many treats feature potatoes: potato skins, french fries, and baked potatoes with yummy toppings. Have the boys and girls search for as many recipes as they can find and compile them into a book. Decorate the cover and pages with potato stamp prints. Include this one:

1/2 cup warm mashed potatoes
1/2 cup peanut butter
1 lb. confectioner's sugar

Mix the sugar with the warm mashed potatoes. Roll out into a rectangle. Spread the peanut butter over that. Roll up like a jelly roll and cut into slices. Serve.

Poem

McGough, Roger. "Potato Clock." In *The Oxford Treasury of Children's Poems*, ed. Michael Harrison and Christopher Stuart-Clark. Oxford University Press, 1988.

Word Play

American speech and culture are filled with potato-related sayings and behaviors:

"That idea is as cold as yesterday's mashed potatoes."
The "Mashed Potato" was a popular dance of the sixties.
"Do you watch too much television? Are you a couch potato?"

Read More About It

Johnson, Sylvia. *Potatoes*. Lerner, 1984. 48 pp. (I).

Leedy, Loreen. *The Potato Party and Other Troll Tales*. Holiday House, 1989. 32 pp. (P).

McDonald, Megan. *The Potato Man*. Orchard, 1991. 32 pp. (P-I). Illustrated by Ted Lewin.

Turner, Dorothy. *Potatoes*. Carolrhoda, 1989. 32 pp. (P).

Watts, Barrie. *Potato*. Silver Burdett, 1988. 25 pp. (P-I).

4.5 Corn

Politi, Leo. *Three Stalks of Corn*. Scribner's, 1993. 32 pp. (P-I).

In Pico Rivera, California, Angelica lives with her *abuelita*, Mrs. Corrales. Grandmother likes to garden; she plants all the ingredients, including corn, needed for the Mexican food that she makes so well. Mrs. Corrales passes on the rich Hispanic culture and customs to her grandaughter. She tells her the ancient legends of Mexico, especially those related to corn. She teaches Angelica how to make hot chocolate, tortillas, tacos, and enchiladas. The school principal invites Angelica's *abuelita* to show the other children how to make tortillas and tacos. Recipes for these are included.

Gardening Activity

Plant a Corn Field

Plant several varieties of corn, such as strawberry, blue, popcorn, Indian, giant, or sweet. For seeds of giant corn, write for a seed catalog from:

Gurney's Seed Nursery Co.
110 Capital St.
Yankton, SD 57079

Try experimenting with growing corn in plastic buckets as suggested in Selsam's book *Popcorn*.

Language Arts Activity

Five Senses Stories

Popping popcorn appeals to all five senses, so it's one of the best stimuli for a five senses chart, which in turn can become a springboard into creative writing. Distribute a five senses chart and ask your boys and girls to pay attention to words that come into their minds while the corn is popping. Ask them to be aware of the sights, sounds, smells, textures, and tastes of popping and popped corn. After their charts are filled with words in each category, have them write a story suggested to them by their charts. After the writing has been shared, edited, and rewritten, display the finished products in a class book, class magazine, or on a bulletin board in the classroom, library, or media center.

Creative Activity

Corn Husk Wreaths

Save the husks from sweet corn. While they are fresh, green, and pliable, use them to create a wreath. Bend wire (a wire coat hanger is just right) into a circle. Fold a husk so that a loop is formed. Lap the loop over the wire. Bring the two ends of the husk up and through the loop. Pull the ends so that a snug knot is formed. Repeat this process until the wire is covered with knotted husks. With a pin, shred the husk so you have a brushy effect. Embellish the wreath with found items from the garden or a nature walk.

Directions for making corn husk wreaths may also be found in *Corn Is Maize*. by Aliki.

Treat

Mexican Corn Bread

3/4 cup sugar
1/2 cup of margarine
1 4-ounce can minced green chilies
1 15-ounce can creamed corn
1/2 cup grated jack cheese
1/2 cup grated cheddar cheese

1 cup flour
1 cup corn meal
4 tsp. baking powder
1/4 tsp. salt
4 beaten eggs

Cream the sugar and margarine together. Stir in corn, chilies, and grated cheeses. Sift together the flour, corn meal, baking powder, and salt. Add this to the corn and chilies mixture. Add the eggs and beat. Pour into two greased loaf pans. Bake at 375° for 40 minutes. This bread freezes well.

You may wish to serve this treat on August 1, which in ancient British culture marked the midpoint, or cross-quarter day, between the Summer solstice and the Autumn equinox and was a day of celebration called Lamas.

Poem

Richards, Laura. "The Song of the Corn-Popper." In *Tirra Lirra*. Little, Brown, 1902.

Word Play

When people think that something is not very sophisticated, they say, "That's corny!" An old saying about corn growing is, "Knee high by the Fourth of July."

Read More About It

Aliki. *Corn Is Maize*. Crowell, 1976. 34 pp. (P).

de Paola, Tomie. *The Popcorn Book*. Holiday House, 1975. 32 pp. (I).

Kellogg, Cynthia. *Corn: What It Is, What It Does*. Greenwillow, 1989. 47 pp. (P).

Selsam, Millicent. *Popcorn*. Morrow, 1976. 48 pp. (P).

Woodside, Dave. *What Makes Popcorn Pop?* Atheneum, 1980. 74 pp. (I).

Chapter 5
Fruit

As with the unit on vegetables, this unit is also not a "Do it in a day" project. For most situations it will be best to read the featured book, plant the tree or bush in the Spring, and then follow up in the Summer or Autumn by rereading the book and doing the activities when the featured fruit is more readily available.

The fruits featured in these units are: apples, peaches, cherries, strawberries, and blueberries. You may want to create your own unit based on local crops and locally available books that are published regionally. Ask for help from your local librarians, orchardists, Master Gardeners, and Cooperative Extension Agents.

Further, this unit provides you with the chance to study various cultures. Japanese and Chinese folktales include peach referents. An inner-city African American girl is the heroine of *Cherries and Cherry Pits*. An ancient Cherokee tale tells of the first strawberries.

5.1 Apples

Patent, Dorothy Hinshaw. *An Apple a Day: From Orchard to You.* Cobblehill, 1990. 64 pp. (I).

Through the color photographs by William Munoz and a clearly written text, readers learn the step-by-step process of propagating, grafting, cultivating, pruning, and harvesting apples. Apple varieties are described. The history of apples as well as their commercial uses today are recounted.

Gardening Activity

Grafting

Grafting is an important method for producing more apple trees. Invite an orchardist or Master Gardener to speak to your group about grafting. Request that he bring sufficient number of branches, tender shoots, and tape so your children can try their hand at grafting. Depending on the ages of your boys and girls, some may need the cutting done for them.

If possible, grow a miniature apple tree in a large tub. One possible source is:

Stark Brothers Nurseries
P.O. Box 10, Highway 54 West
Louisiana, MO 63353-0010

Have your children write a letter requesting their catalog.

Language Arts Activity

Apple Cubing

Cubing is a prewriting activity. Cubing is a way to encourage young writers to think about a topic, organize their thoughts, and begin to write about it. Draw a large empty cross on mural paper, dividing it into six 18-inch squares, one on each of the side arms, one at the top, one in the center, and two on the bottom portion of the cross as in figure 5.1.

In each of the squares have the children write a sentence or two as indicated. Lead your group through the following six steps to think and write about the topic "Apples":

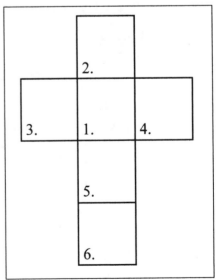

Fig. 5.1. Sample cube.

In square 1 write a sentence or two that describes apples.

In square 2 write what apples remind you of.

In square 3 compare apples to another fruit.

In square 4 write a detailed sentence that tells about the different characteristics of apples.

In square 5 write what apples may be used for.

In square 6 write why you like or dislike apples.

Have the children cut out their cross, fold it, and form it into a cube. Have them glue it together. As a final step, have them write a composition about apples.

Creative Activity

Dried Apple Wreaths

Have these materials on hand:

an anti-browning fruit protector product (ascorbic acid, Fruit Fresh®, or salt and lemon juice mixture)

12 apples per wreath

cardboard

tacky glue

wire baking racks

cookie sheets

Read or tell the following directions.

Drying the apples:

1. Slice the apples into ⅛" slices.

2. Dip each slice into an anti-browning mixture.

3. Pat dry.

4. Spread on wire baking racks.

5. Place the racks on cookie sheets.

6. Dry in a 140° oven for up to six hours, but check them after five hours. The slices should be leathery and dry all over.

Making the wreath:

1. Cut a wreath shape out of the cardboard square.

2. Glue the apples onto the cardboard wreath, overlapping the apple slices slightly.

Treat

Applesauce

Fresh apples make a delicious treat as is. However, for a more elaborate treat, read Johnson's *Apples to Applesauce* to your group and follow her recipe or one of your own. Here's another to choose from:

Eight apples, washed, cored, quartered but not pared

Enough water to keep the apples from burning

Place in a saucepan and cook on medium heat until the apples are soft. Push through a strainer or a food mill. Season with sugar, salt, butter, and cinnamon to taste.

(You may wish to take advantage of a teachable moment here, to talk about fractions: halves and quarters as the apples are being prepared.)

Poem

Ousley, Odille. "If I Were an Apple." In *V Is for Verses*. Ginn, 1964.

Word Play

Here are some common idiomatic expressions:

"That's as American as apple pie."
"She's the apple of my eye."
"How do you like them apples!"

Read More About It

Bougeois, Paulette. *The Amazing Apple*. Addison-Wesley, 1990. 64 pp. (P-I).

Johnson, Hannah. *From Appleseed to Applesauce*. Lothrop, Lee & Shepard, 1977. 44 pp. (P-I).

Miccucci, Charles. *The Life and Times of the Apple*. Orchard, 1992. 32 pp. (P-I).

Priceman, Marjorie. *How to Make an Apple Pie and See the World*. Knopf, 1994. 32 pp. (P-I).

Slawson, Michele Benoit, and Deborah Kogan Ray. *Apple Picking Time*. Crown, 1994. 32 pp. (P).

5.2 Peaches

Motomara, Mitchell. *Momotaro*. Raintree, 1989. 32 pp. (P). Illustrated by Kyuzo Tsugami.

In this Japanese folktale a childless couple is delighted to find a baby boy in a giant peach. They name their child Momotaro. All live happily until ogres invade their village and steal all their belongings. Momotaro pursues the ogres to their homeland. With the aid of a dog, a monkey, and a pheasant, he overcomes the ogres and retrieves the family's possessions.

Gardening Activity

Investigating Peach Culture

If possible, take a field trip to a peach orchard in the Spring when it is blooming and in the late Summer when the peaches are being harvested. Invite a commercial orchardist or a knowledgeable home orchardist to speak to your group. Have the children ask questions like these and others of their own:

What are the different varieties of peaches?

What is the difference between freestone and clingstone?

How are peaches propagated?

How are new varieties developed?

What kind of care do peach trees require?

What kinds of sprays are used on peach trees? Why?

How many times a year are the trees sprayed?

What pests and diseases are peach trees subject to?

How are peach trees pruned? Why?

If possible, ask the speaker to teach your boys and girls to prune a peach tree. If possible, plant a peach whip.

Language Arts Activity

Peach Pit Board Game

Materials:

File folders

peach pits

colored markers

index cards

pencils

Have your youngsters create file folder board games based on their knowledge about peaches, peach trees, and peach tree cultivation. Have them write a question about peaches on the front of an index card and write the answer on the back. Have them give a value from one to three to each question. This value determines how many spaces a player may move. Twenty to thirty questions make a reasonable game. Have them draw a segmented track that shows where to start and stop the game on their file folders with the colored markers. Encourage creativity related to the imaginary setting of the track; what penalties and bonuses could be built into the track; the illustrations and decorations that might be drawn on the file folder.

Allow time for the games to be played. Each player uses a peach pit as a marker.

As a variation, some youngsters could make up a board game based on the Momotaro story.

Creative Activity

Peach Pit Jewelry

Peach pits make great jewelry for the children and gifts for their friends and relatives. Peach pits may be made into key rings, necklaces, pins, and the like. Gather and save many peach pits over time. Have on hand white glue, elastic thread or narrow bands, velvet or grosgrain ribbon, water-base enamel paint, acrylics, tempera paint, brushes of various sizes and a hand drill with a $1/16$" wood bit (you may want bits of more than one size depending on the width of the ribbons and threads). Have the boys and girls experiment with drilling, painting, glueing, and designing peach pit pins, bracelets, and necklaces.

Be sure to talk with them about the safe use of tools and remind them to wear safety glasses when drilling the peach pits. It's not too early to develop safe work habits.

Treat

Peach Leather

Distribute fresh peaches for the treat or make peach leather.

Gather eight ripe peaches, peel and remove the stones.

Place in a blender and blend until smooth.

Pour onto the prepared cookie sheets.

Spread evenly so that it is about 1/16-inch thick over all.

Place into a warm oven for about seven hours. Check on the leather after five hours. The leather should feel tacky to the touch. If left to dry too long, it will become brittle rather than leathery.

You may prefer to dry the peaches with a solar method by leaving the cookie sheets in the sunlight for about seven hours. Be sure to cover the leather with cheesecloth so the insects don't help themselves to lunch.

Poem

Anonymous. "Petals." In *Shades of Green*, Anne Harvey. Greenwillow, 1991.

Word Play

When we like something, we say, "That's peachy."

A young girl's smooth complexion is sometimes described as being like peaches and cream.

When the first signs of a young man's beard appears, he is sometimes kidded about his "peach fuzz."

Read More About It

Bordewich, Fergus M. *Peach Blossom Spring*. Green Tiger, 1994. 42 pp. (P-I).

Manton, Jo, and Robert Gittings. "The Peach Blossom Forest." In *The Flying Horses*. Holt, Rinehart & Winston, 1977. pp. 75-82. (I).

Pike, Norman. *The Peach Tree*. Stemmer, 1983. 32 pp. (P).

Sakade, Florence. "Peach Boy." In *Favorite Japanese Stories*. Charles E. Tuttle, 1958. 120 pp. (I).

Tabrah, Ruth, ed. *Momotaro*. Island Heritage, 1992. 60 pp. (I).

Zimmelman, Nathan. *I Will Tell You of Peach Stone*. Lothrop, Lee & Shepard, 1976. 26 pp. (P). Illustrated by Haru Wells.

5.3 Cherries

Williams, Vera B. *Cherries and Cherry Pits*. Greenwillow, 1986. 36 pp. (P).

Bidemmi loves to color; she loves to draw; she loves to tell stories. With her markers she draws pictures about which she begins to tell stories with the word "This."

She draws pictures and tells stories about people who like to eat cherries. Her last story is about herself planting the cherry pits that will sprout into trees. As Bidemmi says, "I know that if I plant enough of them at least one cherry tree will grow." She imagines the future and all her friends enjoying her cherry forest.

This book is perfect for youth leaders, teachers, and librarians looking for a way to motivate children to write. They may be encouraged to start their stories just as Bidemmi did, with "This." Often in gardening and botany classes students are asked to draw a series of pictures showing what is occurring to a plant over time. Bidemmi shows us how to do this.

Gardening Activity

Plant Cherry Trees

Plant one tree if it is a sour cherry tree, two trees if you want to harvest sweet cherries because these need a pollinator tree. You may wish to combine this tree-planting activity with your Arbor Day event. Invite a hobby or commercial orchardist or local nursery employee to assist with this project. Have a discussion with the orchardist and the children about these questions: What is our agricultural zone? What are the implications of that fact? What are the soil conditions in our area? Where will the tree be planted? How much sun will it get?

What is the water source for the tree? How big should the hole be dug? What varieties of cherry trees grow well in our area? What type of tree do we want to plant: sweet cherry, sour, ornamental, or weeping? Does this variety call for special treatment, such as needing a pollinator tree planted close by?

Other questions to be considered: What is the purpose of the tree? Who will benefit from it? What is needed at a particular spot? For example, you may find out that a local nursing home could use an ornamental cherry in its patio area. Or that a shut-in would enjoy a cherry tree outside his/her window. Or that the city park needs to replace a tree damaged by vandalism.

Language Arts Activity

Bidemmi Pictures

Bidemmi loves her markers and she loves to tell stories about people who fascinate her. She asks the fiction writer's question, "What would happen if. . . ." Take your group of boys and girls to a great spot for people watching. Supply them with drawing boards, paper, and markers (*EcoArt* by Carlson has ideas for portable drawing boards). Have them draw a series of pictures showing what would happen if (the person they spotted) did (whatever). Having bags of sweet cherries or other fruit to nibble while drawing would be fun. Don't forget to plant and water the pits.

Creative Activity

Sweet and Sour Board Game

Preparation: With tempera paint or colored markers color 32 cherry pits, 16 black and 16 red. Duplicate the Sweet and Sour game board in this chapter. You may want to enlarge it. If left the original size, it fits into a file folder for easy storage. Glue the game board onto tagboard to reinforce it. Duplicate the following directions onto an index card.

Directions for Sweet and Sour

Attention: This game uses positive and negative numbers. If your children do not know what this means, explain it to them.

Number of players: 4

Object: To be the first player to circle the board and return to the Start space.

Materials: Game board (fig. 5.2 on page 67) and 4 black cherry pits and 4 red cherry pits for each player. Four clean 6-ounce frozen fruit juice cans.

To start the game: Each player in turn shakes his or her pits inside the can and then tosses the pits into the circle and counts all of the ones that landed within the circle. The person to have the lowest number land within the circle begins the game.

Method of play: The black pits represent sweet cherries; they have positive numbers. The red pits represent sour cherries; they have negative numbers.

Each player selects four black pits and four red pits. When it is a player's turn, he/she shakes and tosses the eight pits into the center of the board. Ignoring the pits that land outside of the center, the player counts the number of black pits within the circle. He or she counts the number of red pits within the circle. The player subtracts the number of red pits from the number of black pits. Examples: 3 black pits minus 2 red pits equals 1. Therefore, the player moves ahead one space. One black pit minus 4 red pits equals -3. Therefore, the player moves backwards three spaces.

Pits that fall on the line are counted as outside the circle.

Play proceeds until a player returns to Start.

Treat

Cherry Crisp

2 pints red sour cherries, drained	1 1/4 cups flour
1 1/4 cups sugar	1 tsp. cinnamon
dash of salt	1/3 cup butter

Check that all the cherry pits have been removed. Dump the cherries into a buttered baking dish. Mix the dry ingredients. Cut in the butter until the mixture is crumbly. Pour the crumb mixture over the cherries. Bake at 375° for an hour.

Poem

Rossetti, Christina. "Oh, Fair to See." In *A Child's Book of Poems*. Grosset & Dunlap, 1974. Illustrated by Gyo Fujikawa.

Fig. 5.2. Sweet and Sour game board.

 **Word Play**

When we are in a good mood and feeling optimistic about life, we say, "Life is just a bowl of cherries."

Read More About It

Balan, Bruce. *The Cherry Migration*. Green Tiger Press, 1988, 32 pp. (P). Illustrated by Dan Lane.

Beck, Barbara. *The First Book of Fruits*. Watts, 1976. 64 pp. (I).

Ikeda, Daisaku. *The Cherry Tree*. Knopf, 1992. 32 pp. (P). Illustrated by Brian Wildsmith.

Laird, Elizabeth. "Cherry Ripe." In *Rosy's Garden*. Philomel, 1990. pp. 30-31. (P-I). Illustrated by Satomi Ichikawa.

Namioka, Lensey. *Valley of the Broken Cherry Trees*. Delacorte, 1980. 218 pp. (I).

Petie, Haris. *The Seed the Squirrel Dropped*. Prentice-Hall, 1976. 32 pp. (P).

5.4 Strawberries

Bruchac, Joseph. *The First Strawberries: A Cherokee Story*. Dial, 1993. 30 pp. (P-I). Illustrated by Anna Vojtech.

The first man and the first woman were living quite happily together until one day the man came home to find that his supper was not ready. The first woman was out picking flowers. A quarrel broke out between them and the first woman walked away from the first man toward the sun. The man followed but could not catch up with her. The sun said that he would help the man because he had said that he was sorry for his harsh words. The sun shone hard. Where it shone, raspberries, then blueberries, then blackberries sprang up but the woman kept on walking. Finally the sun shone as hard as it could and there strawberries grew. The woman stopped to pick them. When she tasted one she was reminded of the sweetness she had had with the first man. She picked them as a peace offering to give to the first man.

Gardening Activity

Strawberry Pots and Patches

Raise strawberries in a half-barrel, strawberry pot, tower, pyramid, or plot depending on your circumstances.

If you have enough land, plant a strawberry patch. Call your county agriculture agent to learn which varieties grow best in your area. Be sure to mulch after the plants have been planted. Strawberries love water so don't let them dry out. Later, point out to your youngsters the runners sent out by the strawberry plant.

Excellent directions for growing strawberries can be found on pages 76 and 77 of Sunset's *Best Kids Gardening Book.*

Language Arts Activity

Storytelling

Have your boys and girls learn the story *The First Strawberries* for storytelling. Write these 10 steps for learning a story on a poster to help them learn it.

1. Select a story that you love.

2. Read the story to yourself about five times.

3. Note the main events of the story.

4. Visualize the characters. Tell yourself what they look like and how they feel.

5. Visualize the main events. Close your eyes and see them going by like a movie.

6. On adding-machine tape, draw sketches of the main scenes and events of the story.

7. Tell the story to yourself over and over and over again.

8. Tell the story by yourself in front of a mirror.

9. Tell your story to a very good listener.

10. Tell your story to a group of children.

Creative Activity

Creative Movement

Using Native American flute music as background, try wordless creative movement with your group to pantomime and dramatize the story of *The First Strawberries*. The story could be enacted through a simple creative dance that the children, working in groups of three, could create.

Treat

Fresh Strawberries

Serve fresh strawberries, preferably ones from the children's garden.

Poem

Field, Rachel. "Wood-strawberries." In *Taxis and Toadstools*. Doubleday & Doran, 1945.

Word Play

The strawberry gets its name from its growing habit. The strawberry sends out runners that appear to be "straying" from the main plant; thus, it was originally called a strayberry. Over the years the pronunciation has been modified.

Read More About It

Bang, Molly. *The Grey Lady and the Strawberry Snatcher*. Four Winds Press, 1980. 48 pp. (P-I).

Degan, Bruce. *Jamberry*. Harper, 1983. 32 pp. (P).

Lenski, Lois. *Strawberry Girl*. Dell, 1945. 195 pp. (I).

Sunset Editors. *Best Kids Garden Book*. Sunset, 1992. pp. 76-77. (P-I).

Wood, Don, and Audrey Wood. *The Little Mouse, the Red Ripe Strawberry, and the Big Hungry Bear*. Child's Play, 1984. 32 pp. (P).

5.5 Blueberries

McCloskey, Robert. *Blueberries for Sal*. Viking, 1948. 54 pp. (P).

Little Sal and her mother and Little Bear and his mother went off for a day of blueberry gathering and eating. Each offspring becomes separated from their mothers and gets mixed up; however, they get back together in time to go back to their homes. Robert McCloskey's ageless charming drawings keep this picture book a delight to this day.

Gardening Activity

Grow Blueberries

Blueberries require acid soil. The soil must have a pH between 4 and 5; they will not thrive if the pH falls below 4. If you have the right conditions, plant and cultivate several bushes. If you live where the soil is alkaline, dig out a hole or trench and replace the soil with a mixture of one part of the original soil to which aluminum sulfate has been added; two parts of soil for rhododendrons, azaleas, and blueberries; two parts of a mixture of coffee grounds, ground-up lemon, and grapefruit peels and/or pine needles to provide acidity; and one part sand to provide drainage. Test the soil to be sure it is the proper pH. You could also place this soil mixture in a very large container such as a half-barrel. Plant and care for the blueberry bushes. It is important to obtain varieties suited for either the North or the South. Blueberry bushes for cultivation may be obtained by mail order from:

Stark Brothers Nurseries
P.O. Box 10, Highway 54 West
Louisiana, MO 63353-0010

Park Seed
Cokesbury Rd.
Greenwood, SC 29647-0001

Language Arts Activity

Poems from a Pattern

Read aloud Bruce Degan's *Jamberry* to your group. Invite your girls and boys to write their own berry verses using the pattern established by the poem.

Creative Activity

Dyeing Cloth and Making a Stuffed Toy

Blueberries make excellent blue dye. Have your children dye scraps of woven, not knit, cloth (an old pillowcase, a faded cotton shirt that is worn out). Just be sure to have enough to make a stuffed toy.

Have these materials on hand to make the dye:	And these materials for the toys:
1 pint blueberries	½ yard scrap cotton material
water	needle
an enamel pot	thread
cheese cloth	2 buttons
potato masher	pattern (fig. 5.3 on page 72)
alum	

Fig. 5.3. Blue Bearee pattern.

From *Beyond the Bean Seed*. © 1996. Nancy Allen Jurenka and Rosanne J. Blass. Teacher Ideas Press. (800) 237-6124.

To make dye from blueberries:

Using an enamel pan, boil berries in enough water to cover for a minute. Let them steep. Mash with a potato masher and strain through cheese cloth. Add 1 teaspoon of alum as a mordant. Immerse the cloth to be dyed into the dye. Let it soak for a few minutes. Wring out and hang up to dry.

To make the stuffed toy:

Using the pattern given, make Blue Bearee with the dyed cloth. Duplicate enough patterns for your group. Have them cut out two pieces from the same pattern, a front and a back. On the front piece have them sew on buttons for eyes. Have them embroider a smile with an outline stitch. Cover the front piece with the back piece (the inside will be facing out). Stitch Blue Bearee closed with a blanket stitch, leaving an opening to use for stuffing. Turn the toy inside out. Stuff Blue Bearee with strips of cloth rags. Stitch the opening shut.

Treat

Blueberry Muffins

1 cup flour	1/2 cup milk
1 1/2 tsp. baking powder	1 egg beaten
1 Tbs. sugar	2 Tbs. melted
1/2 cup fresh blueberries	margarine

Sift the dry ingredients together. Mix the milk, egg, and margarine. Pour into the flour mixture. Stir in the blueberries. Pour into muffin tins. Bake at 400° for 15 to 20 minutes.

Poem

Eastwick, Ivy. "Berries." In *Sprouts of Green: Poems for Young Gardeners*, by Ella Bramblett. Crowell, 1968.

Read More About It

Beskow, Elsa. *Peter in Blueberry Land.* Floris Books, 1987. 32 pp. (P-I).

Degan, Bruce. *Jamberry.* Harper, 1983. 32 pp. (P).

Dowden, Anne Ophelia. *From Flower to Fruit.* Tichnor & Fields, 1994. 56 pp. (I).

Fenton, Carroll Lane, and Herminie Kitchen. *Fruits We Eat.* John Day, 1961. 128 pp. (I).

Lember, Barbara Hirsch. *A Book of Fruit.* Tichnor and Fields, 1994. 32 pp. (P).

Mintz, Lorelie. *How to Grow Fruits and Berries.* Messner, 1980. 96 pp. (I).

Chapter 6
Plant Variety

Not every plant a child may be interested in learning about is a pretty flower or tasty vegetable. Here are books and activities related to mushrooms, toadstools, fungi, ferns, cacti, carnivorous plants, and trees.

These books will transport children to deep forests, swamps, deserts, and mountains as they learn of the various habitats and habits of the great variety of plants on our planet. They will be taken back in time to dinosaur times to learn about ferns.

Most of these activities may be done at times other than Summer so they provide you with subjects to study and things to do with plants when Autumn, Spring, or Winter keeps your group indoors.

6.1 Mushrooms and Molds: The Fungi Family

Johnson, Sylvia. *Mushrooms*. Lerner, 1982. 48 pp. (I).

Photos, diagrams, and text provide information about some of the more than 38,000 different kinds of mushrooms. Mushrooms belong to the fungi family, a group of plants that do not make their own food. This book explains how mushrooms get their food, grow, and reproduce. Many mushrooms are edible; some are poisonous. Scientific and common names are given. Of particular interest is the explanation of mushroom fairy rings.

Gardening Activity

Grow Bread Mold

Read these directions to your group:

Experiment with bread to identify conditions that favor mold growth. Begin with eight pieces of bread. Seal one moist piece of bread in plastic wrap; expose another to the air. Place one piece of bread in bright light; another in the dark. Let one piece dry out while you keep another piece moist. Place one piece of bread in a warm dark place such as an oven. Place another in a cold dark place such as a refrigerator. Use a magnifying glass or jeweler's loupe to examine the bread daily. Record changes that you see.

Language Arts Activity

Retelling

Use the series of six photos at the end of Barrie Watts's *Mushrooms* to sequence a retelling of the story of a mushroom's growth. Illustrate your retelling with your own pictures.

Creative Activity

Spore Prints

Provide your group with these directions:

Gather mushrooms or buy mushrooms at the supermarket. Cut the caps off the stems. Place caps on pieces of paper with gills facing downward. If you have gathered wild mushrooms, be certain not to touch your mouth with your hands and be certain to wash your hands as a precaution against ingesting poisonous material. Let the mushroom caps sit overnight. When you remove the mushroom caps hours later, you will have spore prints.

Treat

Mushroom Salad

Sample edible mushrooms by serving Mushroom Salad. Wash and dry spinach or lettuce leaves. Top with cleaned, sliced mushrooms. Add a salad dressing of your choice.

Poem

Spilka, Arnold. "Mushrooms Are Umbrellas." In *The Earth Is Painted Green*, by Barbara Brenner. Scholastic, 1994.

Word Play

Some fungi have descriptive common names, such as turkey tail, bear's head fungus, and jelly babies.

Read More About It

Burnie, David. *How Nature Works: 100 Ways Parents and Kids Can Share the Secrets of Nature.* Reader's Digest, 1991. 192 pp. (I).

Froman, Robert. *Mushrooms and Molds.* Crowell, 1972. 32 pp. (P).

Heller, Ruth. *Plants That Never Bloom.* Sandcastle, 1984. 44 pp. (P-I).

Selsam, Millicent. *Mushrooms.* Morrow, 1986. 48 pp. (P-I).

Watts, Barrie. *Mushroom.* Silver Burdett, 1986. 24 pp. (P).

6.2 Ferns and Friends: Dinosaur Plants

Wexler, Jerome. *From Spore to Spore: Ferns and How They Grow*. Dodd, Mead, 1985. 48 pp. (P-I).

Although life on earth has changed, ferns have changed very little since the age of dinosaurs. Whether the soil is acid or alkaline, rock, clay, or sand, ferns thrive with plenty of moisture and mild temperatures in full sun or shade. They can be found around the world in such places as the United States, Central America, and New Zealand. Text and photos trace the life cycle of ferns and give advice on growing them. This book concludes with names of fern societies that you can contact for more information.

Gardening Activity

Research and Raise

Ferns reproduce from spores rather than from seeds. They can also be grown from rhizomes, bulbils, and frond tip buds. Research and raise ferns using each method. See Joel Rapp's *Let's Get Growing* for more information.

Language Arts Activity

Read Aloud

Read aloud "The Power of Ferns" from Anne Pellowski, *Hidden Stories in Plants*.

Creative Activity

Spatter Prints

Materials:

> newspaper
>
> white paper
>
> toothbrush
>
> poster paint
>
> popsicle stick

Directions: Cover work space with newspapers. Lay a fern on a piece of white paper. Scrape a toothbrush dipped in poster paint with the popsicle stick until paper is covered with spatter design. Be certain to pull the popsicle stick toward you rather than away from you; otherwise, you will cover yourself with paint and really irritate the person who has to wash your clothes! This is an activity best done outside on a warm Summer day.

Carefully lift fern from paper. Let print dry.

Treat

Fern Fronds

Tender young fern fronds are considered a delicacy.
Gather and serve in early Spring.

Poem

Norris, Leslie. "The Black Fern." In *The Scott Foresman Anthology of Children's Literature*, ed. Zena Sutherland and Myra Cohn Livingston. Scott, Foresman, 1984.

Word Play

Common plant names frequently describe characteristics of plants or refer to something they resemble. A few such names for ferns are cinnamon, fiddle back, and bird's nest.

Read More About It

Heller, Ruth. *Plants That Never Bloom.* Sandcastle, 1984. 44 pp. (P-I).

Kavaler, Lucy. *Green Magic: Algae Rediscovered.* Crowell, 1983. 120 pp. (I).

Rapp, Joel. *Let's Get Growing.* Prince Paperbacks, 1993. 96 pp. (I).

Shuttleworth, Floyd S. *Non-Flowering Plants.* Golden Press, 1967. 159 pp. (P-I).

Sterling, Dorothy. *The Story of Mosses, Ferns, and Mushrooms.* Doubleday, 1955. 159 pp. (P-I).

6.3 Cacti and Succulents: Youngest Plants on Earth

Holmes, Anita. *Cactus: The All-American Plant.* Four Winds, 1982. 192 pp. (I).

The author shares her love for the desert and its many cacti by taking readers on a journey of discovery. Graceful but detailed pencil drawings support the readable and informative text. A comprehensive resource for the novice, this book explains cacti's adaptation to and role in the natural environment, describes cacti's distinguishing characteristics and multiple uses, including recipes for cooking, gives directions for raising cacti, and provides appendices, including a map of North American desert areas, a listing of desert gardens, museums, and natural areas, and a description and classification of plant varieties.

Gardening Activity

Cactus Dish Garden

You will need:

  a bowl

  broken crockery or coarse gravel

  crushed charcoal

  soil mixed with loam

  small decorative items to create a desert scene

  small cacti

Fill bowl to one-third of its depth with broken crockery or coarse gravel.

Add a thin layer of crushed charcoal. Fill with soil to within 1 inch of top. Arrange cacti in soil. Sprinkle crushed charcoal on top of soil after adding plants.

Create a desert scene with small decorative items.

Language Arts Activity

Topics of Interest

The wealth of information contained in Anita Holmes's book lends itself to further study using cooperative groups, either in pairs or small groups. Have the groups explore topics of interest, such as fun and fascinating descriptive names, medicinal uses of plants, cactus cookery, the desert ecosystem, cacti in legends of Central America or early stone carvings of Mexico, and the California cactus industry.

Creative Activity

Topic for Discussion

Anita Holmes quoted a horticulturist as saying the cactus was "America's greatest gift to the horticultural world." Why do you think the horticulturist made this statement? Support your opinions based on what you know about cacti and other plants.

Treat

> ### Prickly Pear Vegetable
>
> Take several tender new leaves of the prickly pear cactus. Carefully remove thorns. Slice and boil in water to cover or fry in a small amount of cooking oil until tender.
>
> You may prefer to prepare one of the recipes from Anita Holmes's book or to serve commercially prepared cactus jelly or candy.

Poem

Prelutsky, Jack. "You Need to Have an Iron Rear." In *New Kid on the Block*. Greenwillow, 1984. 159 pp. (P-I).

Word Play

Common plant names frequently describe characteristics of plants or refer to something they resemble. A few such names for cacti are chilies on a pie plate, touch-me-not, teddy bear, fishhook, pincushions, and strawberries on a hedgehog.

Read More About It

Bash, Barbara. *Desert Giant: The World of the Saguaro Cactus.* Sierra Club, 1989. 32 pp. (P-I).

Busch, Phyllis. *Cactus in the Desert.* Crowell, 1979. 34 pp. (P).

Guiberson, Brenda Z. *Cactus Hotel.* Holt, 1991. 32 pp. (P-I). Illustrated by Megan Lloyd.

Keats, Ezra Jack. *Clementina's Cactus.* Viking, 1982. 32 pp. (P).

Overbeck, Cynthia. *Cactus.* Lerner, 1982. 48 pp. (P-I).

6.4 Carnivorous Plants: Wetland Dwellers

Wexler, Jerome. *Sundew Stranglers: Plants That Eat Insects*. Dutton, 1995. 46 pp. (I).
Fascinating reading even if the idea of insect-eating plants leaves you cold. Wexler's clear explanations and close-up photographs draw the reader into the explanations, experiments, and history of a plant type that grows on every continent except Antarctica. Readers will discover the mechanism by which the sundew captures and digests insects. Wexler tells his readers that sundews are easy to grow and he explains how to do that.

Gardening Activity

Grow Your Own

The Venus's fly trap is an easy-to-grow bulb plant that can be obtained from a local nursery or through a mail order catalog. It grows best with wet roots, high humidity, poor acid soil, and full sunlight. Use a terrarium or glass bowl to create and maintain a humid environment. Mix 1 part African violet soil with 5 parts sphagnum moss and 5 parts clean sand. Place soil and bulb in terrarium or bowl, covering the bulb to the tip. Place in full sunlight and water regularly.

Language Arts Activity

Write for Information

Carnivorous plants are flesh-eating plants; they are also referred to as insectivorous plants, meaning insect-eating plants. They grow in wetlands such as bogs, marshes, swamps, and coastal areas.

For more information about carnivorous plants and their care write to:

Carnivorous Plant Society
c/o Fullerton Arboretum
California State University
Fullerton, CA 92634

As a courtesy, be sure to include a self-addressed, stamped business-size envelope.

Creative Activity

Carnivorous Collages

Collect an assortment of mail order plant catalogs. Create a collage of carnivorous plants by cutting pictures and information from the catalogs.

Treat

Mud Balls

1/2 cup peanut butter   1/2 cup powdered sugar
1/2 cup dry milk   1/2 cup corn flakes
1 Tbs. butter, melted
4 ounces semisweet chocolate, melted

Mix peanut butter, sugar, milk, and cereal together. Add melted butter. Roll dough into balls. Place on foil-covered cookie sheet and refrigerate to chill. Dip chilled balls into cooled, melted chocolate. Refrigerate again until firm. Store in a covered container. Makes 36 mud balls.

Poem

Williams, Terry. "Between Cattails." Scribner's, 1985. Illustrated by Peter Parnall.

Word Play

Large words sometimes may be broken down into meaningful units; for example, "carnivorous" may be broken down into *carni*, which refers to flesh, and *-vorous*, which refers to eat.

Read More About It

Dean, Anabel. *Plants That Eat Insects: A Look at Carnivorous Plants*. Lerner, 1977. 32 pp. (I).

Lerner, Carol. *Pitcher Plants: The Elegant Insect Traps*. Morrow, 1983. 64 pp. (I).

Overbeck, Cynthia. *Carnivorous Plants*. Lerner, 1982. 48 pp. (I).

Pope, Joyce. *Plant Partnerships*. Facts on File, 1990. 62 pp. (I).

Ricciuti, Edward R. *Plants in Danger*. Harper, 1979. 86 pp. (I).

Wexler, Jerome. *Secrets of the Venus's Fly Trap*. Dodd, Mead, 1981. 64 pp. (I).

6.5 Trees

Glaser, Linda. *Tanya's Big Green Dream.* Macmillan, 1994. 47 pp. (I).

Tanya's Earth Day project last year was a bean seed experiment, but this year in fourth grade, she wants to do something beyond a bean seed. She overcomes obstacle after obstacle to raise money to purchase a tree for the city park. Her classmates make her project their project and all work as a team to achieve this goal. The drawings portray multicultural classmates.

Gardening Activity

Plant a Tree

Research the history of Earth Day and Arbor Day and current Earth and Arbor Day practices in your community. Plant a tree for Earth or Arbor Day.

Language Arts Activity

Display

Use *Crinkleroot's Guide to Knowing the Trees,* by Jim Arnosky, to identify trees in your community. Gather a variety of leaves, pine needles, and pine cones. Develop your own display of trees in your community.

Creative Activity

Waxed Leaves

Materials:

leaves

newspaper

floor wax

brush

Spread several thicknesses of newspaper on the floor. Paint each side of the leaves with floor wax. Lay leaves on newspaper to dry for about 10 minutes. When they are dry, spread several thicknesses of newspaper or other paper over the waxed leaves. Place books on top of the newspaper for weight to keep the leaves flat. Let sit overnight. Use the waxed leaves as a border for the bulletin board that displays your leaf and needle collection.

Treat

Lincoln Log

6 ounces sweet chocolate
5 egg yolks
5 egg whites
1 tsp. vanilla

3 Tbs. strong
   coffee
3/4 cup sugar
1 1/2 cups whipped cream

Grease jelly-roll pan and line with buttered waxed paper. Melt chocolate in coffee over low heat. Beat egg yolks, gradually adding sugar. Mix in chocolate. Beat egg whites until stiff and fold into chocolate mixture. Spread on jelly-roll pan. Bake 15 minutes at 350°. Cover with damp cloth and refrigerate 1 hour. Turn cake onto a piece of waxed paper sprinkled with cocoa. Mix whipped cream with vanilla and spread over cake. Roll up the long way by raising the edge of the wax paper.

Poem

Fisher, Aileen. "Pussy Willows." In *Read-Aloud Rhymes for the Very Young*, by Jack Prelutsky. Knopf, 1986. 98 pp.

Word Play

"Up a tree" means "to be in trouble" or in a predicament of some sort. This expression may have come from raccoon hunting. A hunting dog chases the raccoon up a tree, where it is definitely in a lot of trouble.

Read More About It

Arnosky, Jim. *Crinkleroot's Guide to Knowing the Trees*. Bradbury, 1992. 32 pp. (P).

Brenner, Fred, and Mary Garelick. *The Tremendous Tree Book*. Boyds Mills, 1992. 40 pp. (P-I).

Dowden, Anne Ophelia. *The Blossom on the Bough*. Crowell, 1994. 71 pp. (I).

Ehlert, Lois. *Red Leaf, Yellow Leaf*. Harcourt Brace Jovanovich, 1991. 32 pp. (P).

Florian, Douglas. *Discovering Trees*. Aladdin Books, 1990. 32 pp. (P).

Selsam, Millicent. *Tree Flowers*. Morrow, 1984. 32 pp. (P-I). Illustrated by Carol Lerner.

Soutter-Perrot, Andrienne. *The Oak*. Creative Edition, 1993. 32 pp. (P-I).

Wexler, Jerome. *Wonderful Pussy Willows*. Dutton, 1992. 32 pp. (P-I).

Chapter 7
Getting Ready to Garden

This chapter, the centerpiece of this book, emphasizes the notion that successful gardening starts with good soil. The first two lessons, "Soil" and "Compost," focus on how to create productive soil. Children are given guidelines for creating a garden plot in the third set of lessons. The fourth set of lessons in this chapter has children identifying weeds and experimenting with various kinds of mulches. The lessons that follow provide plenty of ways to fill the plot you've prepared.

This set of lessons is best done during the growing season in your part of the country. For groups and classes gardening in California, the South, and Southwest, several full seasons of gardening might be accomplished, starting in March. For school groups gardening in the north, gardening with children may call for starting the garden in the late Spring before school ends and then making arrangements for the garden to be cared for over the Summer. Some schools accomplish this by 1) signing up parents, community volunteers, and children to care for the garden on a scheduled basis; 2) having the care done by the Summer school classes; or 3) enlisting the help of the local garden club, Master Gardeners, or service club members.

7.1 Soil

Wyler, Rose. *Science Fun with Mud and Dirt.* Messner, 1986. 48 pp. (P-I).
In easy-to-understand text, the structure and composition of dirt are detailed. Readers are given experiments to do with dirt. Inhabitants of dirt are described. Projects, such as making mud houses and bricks, are explained. Wyler tells of the importance of soil to human life and explains what boys and girls can do to conserve soil.

Gardening Activity

Soil Preparation and Improvement

Have each member of your group dig a shovelful of soil from various locations. Preferably, one should be from your group's garden site. Study the soil samples and pose these questions to the children:

What color is the soil?

How does it feel when it is squeezed?

What does the soil do when it is squeezed? Does it clump up? Fall apart?

Is it mostly clay, sand, or humus? Is it a balance of those three?

What material needs to be added?

Is it acid, alkaline, or balanced? Test it with litmus paper. Obtain litmus paper from a pharmacy or a science materials supplier, such as:

Carolina Biological Supply Co.
Burlington, NC 27215
    or
Carolina Biological Supply Co.
Gladstone, OR 97027
(503) 656-1641
1-800-547-1733

Put soil samples (about a handful) from various locations around town into 1-quart glass jars. Mix with a jarful of water. Allow to settle. Describe the results and the implications for the gardener. You may also wish to try the soil-testing procedure that uses violets as described on page 29 in Rhoades's book *Garden Crafts for Kids.*

If you have a garden plot, spend some time on soil improvement and amendment with your boys and girls. Most likely you would need to add grass clippings (be sure they have not been treated with an herbicide), leaves, and composted manure to the soil.

Language Arts Activity

Soil Recipe Accordion Books

What kinds of plants need what kinds of soil mixtures? To find out, assemble and read a collection of books that may include the ones listed in "Read More About It," Cutler's *Growing a Garden Indoors or Out*, or Walsh's *A Gardening Book: Indoors and Outdoors.*

Have the children collect soil recipes, paying special attention to which soil is best for particular kinds of plants. Have the boys and girls write out the recipes and bind them into folded paper books.

Have on hand for each child:

a strip of adding machine paper, 3" x 40"

two pieces of cardboard, 4" x 6"

two pieces of pretty paper (wallpaper, wrapping paper, etc.)

white glue

glue brushes

Have the boys and girls fold the paper into accordion folds so that they have eight 5-inch sections. Attach one end to one piece of cardboard. Attach the other end section to the other piece of cardboard.

Have the children write their soil recipes on the pages, decorate the pages, glue the pretty paper on the front and back, and write the title on the front.

 ## Creative Activity

Creating Soil Mixtures

Provide your group with sand, perlite, ordinary soil, finished compost, fertilizer, alfalfa pellets, and vermiculite.

Have them experiment making different kinds of soils. Use these soil mixtures for making comparative studies or hold a "Best Soil" contest. The soil blends could also be packaged in paper grocery bags, decorated with potato prints or pressed botanicals, and given as presents. Have your youngsters experiment with finding the best mixture for cacti, for houseplants, for starting seeds, or for growing tomatoes.

Treat

Chocolate Dirt Cake

From the Chicago Botanical Garden comes this recipe for a favorite treat of volunteers and children who garden there.*

2 8-ounce packages softened cream cheese
2 4-ounce packages instant vanilla pudding
1 cup milk
1/4 pound butter, softened
1 cup powdered sugar
1 72-ounce container nondairy dessert topping
1 20-ounce package chocolate cookies

Combine all ingredients except the cookies. Blend well. Crush the cookies to make dirt. In a clean, clear plastic flowerpot, layer the ingredients in this order: dirt, pudding mixture, dirt, pudding mixture, ending with a dirt layer. Top with a flower or flowers of your choice. Serve using a shiny new trowel.

* If you're looking for a fund-raiser, these make money-attracting items at dessert auctions.

Poem

Boyden, Polly Chase. "Mud." In *A Small Child's Book of Verse,* by Pelagie Doane. Oxford, 1948.

Shacklett, Mildred D. "Mud Cakes." In *A Small Child's Book of Verse*, by Pelagie Doane. Oxford, 1948.

Read More About It

Bourgeois, Paulette. *The Amazing Dirt Book.* Addison-Wesley, 1990. 80 pp. (P).

Fell, Derek. *A Kid's First Book of Gardening.* Running Press, 1989. pp. 7-13. (P-I).

Rhoades, Diane. *Garden Crafts for Kids.* Sterling/Lark, 1995. 144 pp. (I).

Savage, Candace, and Gary Clement. *Get Growing.* Firefly, 1991. 56 pp. (I).

Simon, Seymour. *Beneath Your Feet.* Walker, 1977. 46 pp. (P).

———. *A Handful of Soil.* Hawthorn, 1970. 63 pp. (I).

7.2 Compost

Rockwell, Harlow. *The Compost Heap.* Doubleday, 1974. 24 pp. (P).

Soft illustrations reveal a young boy and his father working through the seasons making and maintaining their compost pile. The preschool set will find composting easy enough for them to do. This picture book is out of print but still available in the picture book section of public and school libraries. There is no current book written exclusively about compost for young readers.

Gardening Activity

Make a Compost Pile

Find a sunny, convenient location for the compost pile. Have your boys and girls bring in grass clippings, leaves, vegetable peelings, wood chips, and manure (not dog or cat). Have them layer these to create the pile. Keep it moist. Have them add to the pile over time. Turn the pile over periodically. Remember to never add meat or fats to the pile.

You may wish to have the group do various experiments and record the progress and results of these experiments. For example, your boys and girls may want to find out what would happen if several compost ingredients were composted separately and then compared. Or various conditions for composting might be compared, such as amount of moisture, length of time exposed to the sun, covered or uncovered, the effect of black plastic. Or have a race to discover who is able to get their set of ingredients to turn into compost the fastest.

Language Arts Activity

Song Lyrics

Listen to *The Garden Song* and then have your children create new lyrics to change it into *The Compost Song. The Garden Song* may be found on the audiotape: *Rosenshontz Tickles You*, available from Lightyear Records (ISBN 1-87949-634-8). The words may also be found in *Guide to Kids' Gardening* by Ocone and Pranis or *Let's Grow!* by Tilgner. Also, *Inch by Inch*, written by David Mallet and illustrated by Ora Eitan, portrays the lyrics and provides the musical score.

Creative Activity

Gifts of Garden Gold

Gather these materials:

grocery bags

ribbons or raffia

garden-related rubber stamps or vegetable stamps

well-inked stamp pads

Have the boys and girls stamp all-over designs onto the grocery bags. Have them fill the bags with completely processed compost from their compost piles and twist the end shut. Have them tie ribbons or raffia around the twisted end. These bags of compost may be given away to a gardening friend or relative who knows the true value of compost—garden gold.

Treat

Twigs and Sticks Pudding

For each serving, mix 1/4 cup of granola with 1/2 cup fruit-flavored yogurt. Serve in paper cups.

Poem

Bacmeister, Rhoda. "Under the Ground." In *A Small Child's Book of Verse*, by Pelagie Doane. Oxford, 1948.

Word Play

Slogans on T-shirts and bumber stickers declare:

"Compost happens"
"Compost because a rind is a terrible thing to waste"
"Compost with a sense of humus"

Read More About It

Applehof, Mary. *Worms Eat My Garbage.* Flower Press, 1982. 100 pp. (I).

Campbell, Stu. *Let It Rot.* Storey Communications, 1991. 152 pp. (I).

Cobb, Vicki. *Lots of Rot.* Lippincott, 1981. 35 pp. (P).

Harmonious Technologies. *Backyard Composting.* Harmonious Press, 1992. 95 pp. (I).

Jobb, Jamie. *My Garden Companion.* Sierra Club, 1977. 350 pp. (I).

Lavies, Bianca. *Compost Critters.* Dutton, 1993. 30 pp. (I).

Mallett, David. *Inch by Inch: The Garden Song.* HarperCollins, 1995. 26 pp. (P). Illustrated by Ora Eitan.

7.3 Kids Gardening

Raferty, Kevin, and Kim G. Raferty. *Kids Gardening: A Kid's Guide to Messing Around in the Dirt.* Klutz, 1989. 87 pp. (P-I).

A light-hearted approach to basic gardening. The tagboard pages and plastic ring binding permit the young gardener to take the book into the garden so they will have it handy. In addition to basic gardening—soil preparation, seed planting, weeding and watering—the book also contains information about scarecrows, worm farms, and kitchen gardening. Plants are partnered with projects; for example, garlic cultivation with plaiting garlic braids.

Gardening Activity

Garden!

Following the lively advice in Raferty's book, the "Guidelines for Gardening" in the Introduction (p. xi), and the other books mentioned in the "Read More About It" section, get out there and garden. Look around for empty spaces, a raised concrete planter, playground corner, tree lawn, garbage bags, or thrown-out tires. Ignore all the voices, including your own, that say, "It can't be done here." Do it anyway. Make a plan with your group about what plants will be grown where. With your boys and girls, prepare the soil by hand-spading it or having it tilled. Be certain that they have removed stones, weeds, and clods of soil. Add amendments such as shredded leaves, fertilizers, compost or composted manure. Have them rake the plot until it is smooth. Following your plan, mark where the various plants are going to be grown. Plant seeds and seedlings. Water and mulch. Have your youngsters water, weed, and fertilize the garden as needed throughout the growing season.

You may wish to use one of the following as a resource:

Bremner, Elizabeth, and John Pusey. *Children's Gardens.*

Ocone, Lynn, with Eve Pranis. *National Gardening Association Guide to Kids' Gardening.*

Tilgner, Linda. *Let's Grow!*

Language Arts Activity

Videotape

Periodically over the growing season have your gang (in the best sense of that word) make a video recording of progress, occurrences, and themes related to your gardening. Later you may wish to show this videotape at a shopping mall or county fair exhibit of your group's or class's gardening project. Here are some ideas of items to videotape:

weather conditions	soil conditions
what's growing	solutions to problems
gadgets invented	progress reports
birds and other visitors	weeds and weed control
pest control ideas	fund raising

Your boys and girls may wish to exchange videoes with others. Names and addresses of gardening video pals may be obtained by writing to:

Larry Johnson
315 Georgia Avenue North
Minneapolis, MN 55427

Be sure to include a SASE or call VIDEO PALS at 1-800-VID-PALS.

See Larry Johnson's article in the National Gardening Association's newsletter *Growing Ideas,* vol. 4, no. 2, April 1993.

Creative Activity

Divergent Thinking

Have a discussion with your children to stimulate divergent thinking about gardening. Have someone write down their solutions.

How can your garden be different from the usual squares or rectangles that are all neatly laid out in rows? Does your situation call for a different or unusual solution? How could your garden be made:

bigger	stacked	shapelier	more useful
smaller	hung up	patterned	more valuable
odd-shaped	richer	more accessible	for less work
higher	more colorful	less accessible	exemplary
lower	varied	more attractive to—	poetic
curved	special	less attractive to—	artistic
erstwhile	musical	resourceful	chaotic
organized	wild	odd	fun
socially responsible	prettier	rounder	specialized

Treat

Marzipan Garden Cake

1 cup almond paste
1 cup confectioner's sugar
2 drops orange-flavored extract

Combine and knead for 20 minutes on a chilled surface, marble if you have it. Form into tiny beet, carrot, onion, cabbage and green bean shapes. Paint appropriately with food color. Don't forget the leaf shapes. Use these to decorate the top of a chocolate sheet cake frosted with chocolate frosting to resemble a stylized vegetable garden with every "vegetable" neatly in its own patch.

Poem

Farjeon, Eleanor. "To Any Garden." In *Shades of Green*, by Anne Harvey. Greenwillow, 1991.

Word Play

"I never promised you a rose garden," is sometimes used when two people are miffed with each other.

In baseball lingo, the outfield is sometimes called the garden and an outfielder is called a gardener.

Read More About It

Bremner, Elizabeth, and John Pusey. *Children's Gardens: A Field Guide for Teachers, Parents, and Volunteers.* University of California Cooperative Extension Common Ground Garden Program, 1990. 186 pp. (I).

Fell, Derek. *A Kid's First Book of Gardening.* Running Press, 1989. 96 pp. (I).

Hershey, Rebecca. *Ready. Set. Grow: A Kid's Guide to Gardening.* Goodyear, 1995. 104 pp. (P-I).

Krementz, Jill. *A Very Young Gardener.* Dial, 1991. 34 pp. (P).

Lottridge, Celia Barker. *One Watermelon Seed.* Oxford, 1986. 24 pp. (P). Illustrated by Karen Patkau.

Mallett, David. *Inch by Inch: The Garden Song.* HarperCollins, 1995. 26 pp. (P).

Rhoades, Diane. *Garden Crafts for Kids: 50 Great Reasons to Get Your Hands Dirty.* Sterling/Lark, 1995. 144 pp. (I).

Stevenson, Peter, and Mike Stevenson. *Farming in Boxes: One Way to Get Started Growing Things.* Scribner, 1976. 64 pp. (I).

Waters, Marjorie. *The Victory Garden Kids' Book.* Globe Pequot, 1994. 148 pp. (I).

7.4 Caring for the Garden

Hershey, Rebecca. *Ready. Set. Grow! A Kid's Guide to Gardening.* Goodyear, 1995. 104 pp. (P-I).

Divided into three parts, *Ready. Set. Grow!* tells children how to garden both indoors and outdoors. Acknowledging the interest nowadays in connecting gardening with children's literature, Hershey includes a reading list with each of her activities. Crafts, activities, and recipes are included in the third part. Caring for the garden, including the use of mulches fits this lesson.

Gardening Activity

Mulch Experiments

Gardeners mulch to control weeds and conserve water. Which type of mulch is best? With your group, conduct an experiment to find out. In the children's garden, set up three to five plots in which various mulches are used; try the usual such as straw, grass clippings, black plastic, and bark. Try the out-of-the-ordinary, such as thrown-away clothing, blankets, used coffee grounds (latte stands have been known to save their old grounds for gardeners), or cocoa bean hulls (if you live near Hershey, Pennsylvania).

Have your boys and girls log the number of weeds per square foot that appear in a certain number of days or the number of days it takes for the soil to become dry down to 1 inch beneath the surface. Discover which material is the most effective mulch. Be sure to account for the thickness of the mulch material.

Language Arts Activity

Foe Files

Have on hand file folders, manilla paper, paper towels, heavy books or a flower press, and transparent tape.

Weeds are a gardener's prime enemy. Weeds compete with garden plants for water and nutrients as well as harbor diseases and harmful insects. Identifying them is the first step in getting rid of them. Have your children pull up and press at least five weeds. Later, have them attach the pressed weeds to manilla paper, identify, and label them.

Have them decorate file folders and place their pressings in their file folder.

Another activity is to learn to identify weeds when they are in their beginning stages of growth.

Creative Activity

How to Cultivate Healthy Relationships and Groups

To cultivate a garden is to care for it so that the plants will live, thrive, and produce. It means to fertilize the plants so they have nutrients that will improve their leaves, blossoms, and stems; to water the garden so the plants will live; to keep it weed-free so the weeds won't compete for the nutrients and water. To cultivate a garden means to keep the plants free from diseases and pests that will attack and kill the plant; to protect the plants from their enemies.

How is caring for friendships, relationships, and groups the same as caring for a garden? How do we keep groups healthy, together, growing, and producing?

Have your boys and girls discuss these topics within smaller groups; perhaps each group could discuss one topic and synthesize their ideas. Then meet again as one large group to share their ideas and to fill out the chart below. Duplicate the chart on the chalkboard or on chart paper to facilitate the discussion.

What Do These Groups Need to Survive and Grow?

	Caring Needs	Growth Needs	Protection Needs	Cohesion Needs
Friendships				
Families				
Schools				
Our garden group				

End the discussion by saying, "Families, friendships, and groups have special needs in order to survive and thrive just as gardens do. We have discovered a few of them here today. As you go about the business of helping groups thrive in the coming weeks and months, think of other ways to keep relationships healthy and how caring for a garden is similar to caring for a friendship."

Treat

Three Mulch Cake

Make and frost a sheet cake. Mark off three sections in the frosting. Using toasted coconut, toasted slivered almonds, and drained, chopped maraschino cherries, cover the top and sides of the cake by thirds.

Poem

Kumin, Maxine. "Song of the Weeds." In *Anthology of Children's Literature*, ed. Edna Johnson, Evelyn Sickels, and Frances Clarke Sayres, 4th Ed. Houghton Mifflin, 1970.

Word Play

When a grown-up, usually a relative, sees a child that they haven't seen for a while, they might exclaim, "My, my, you've grown like a weed!"

Read More About It

Daddona, Mark. *Hoe, Hoe, Hoe! Watch My Garden Grow.* Addison-Wesley, 1980. 58 pp. (P).

Raferty, Kevin, and Kim G. Raferty. *Kids Gardening: A Kid's Guide to Messing Around in the Dirt.* Klutz, 1989. 87 pp. (P-I).

Rapp, Joel. *Let's Get Growing.* Prince Paperbacks, 1993. 96 pp. (I).

Rhoades, Diane. *Garden Crafts for Kids: 50 Great Reasons to Get Your Hands Dirty.* Sterling/Lark, 1995. 144 pp. (I).

Sunset Editors. *Best Kids Garden Book.* Sunset, 1992. 96 pp. (I).

Waters, Marjorie. *The Victory Garden Kids' Book.* Globe Pequot, 1994. pp. 57-58, 93, 107. (I).

7.5 Plant and Transplant

Porter, Wes. *The Garden Book*. Workman, 1989. 64 pp. (P-I).

In this kid-size book pages 12 through 19 give the low down on the sequence of planting seeds in flats, transplanting the seedlings to containers, followed by transplanting the seedlings into gardens.

The advice is sound. It comes from one of Canada's leading gardening experts who has his own television show. In addition to information about transplanting, Porter tells how to create productive soil, how pollination works, how to plan a garden, and how to care for it once it is planted. He also includes a section on house plants and terrariums.

Gardening Activity

Plant and Transplant

What is the date of the last frost in your area? Have your boys and girls study a United States Department of Agriculture map and determine the date. Count back eight weeks from that date. On that date, have the group plant seeds in various containers (flats, egg cartons, yogurt cartons).

It would be a good time to experiment with one of the soil mixtures mentioned earlier. Place the containers in a sunny window or under a plant light. Keep moist, but not wet. Observe the plant's growth (a good time for journal keeping).

Fertilize the seedlings with a weak solution of liquid fertilizer after they've sprouted. Keep them in a sunny spot and keep them moist. A week before transplanting day, take them outside to get used to outside conditions. This is called hardening off the plants.

Have your youngsters prepare the garden bed to receive the transplants. Dig in some compost. Dig a hole large enough to hold the plant at the same level in the ground as it is in its container. Plant and water the seedlings.

Language Arts Activity

Gardener's Notes

Duplicate the "Gardener's Notes" in figure 7.1 on page 100. Have about 12 for each boy and girl. Bind into a booklet.

Have your boys and girls keep a record of the progress of their transplants in a systematic manner.

Gardener's Notes: _____

_____

Week of: _____

Goals: _____   Date Accomplished: _____

_____   _____

_____   _____

_____   _____

_____   _____

Record here your ideas for projects, chores, and learnings.

_____

_____

_____

_____

_____

_____

_____

_____

Seed List: _____

_____

Weather: _____

_____

Progress Noted: _____

_____

Articles Read: _____

_____

Visitors: _____

_____

Fig. 7.1. Gardener's notes.

Creative Activity

Transplanter's Pocket

Transplanters require tools, dibbles, labels, sticks, and markers. How to hang on to them and keep your hands free is tricky. One solution is a transplanter's pocket. Here's how to make one. Have on hand:

½ yard of rugged fabric such as corduroy or denim

⅓ yard of fabric such as percale for the lining

bias tape (optional)

pattern

Velcro®

shears

pins and needles

thread

1. Using the pattern (fig. 7.2 on page 102), cut two pieces out of denim, suede cloth, or corduroy.

2. Cut two pieces of lining fabric (calico, plaid flannel).

3. With wrong sides together, stitch lining pieces to the front and back pieces using ¼" seam allowance.

4. With the lining sides together, place the pocket front on top of the pocket back. Pin. Stitch together with a blanket stitch, leaving the top open.

5. Optional: Bind edge with bias tape.

6. Make a belt by cutting two strips of matching material each 2¾" by 15".

7. Fold in half with right sides together. Stitch the long side. Now you have a tube. Here's the tricky part. Turn the belt inside out by tucking one end into the inside of the tube and pushing that end through to the other end. It helps to attach a big safety pin to the end so you have something to wiggle through the tube. Press the tube flat with a warm iron.

8. Attach the pocket to the belt by sewing the top edge of the back section of the pocket to the belt so that the pocket is positioned in a convenient spot.

9. Try on for fit.

10. Sew Velcro tabs to the back of each end of the belt. Trim and sew shut each end.

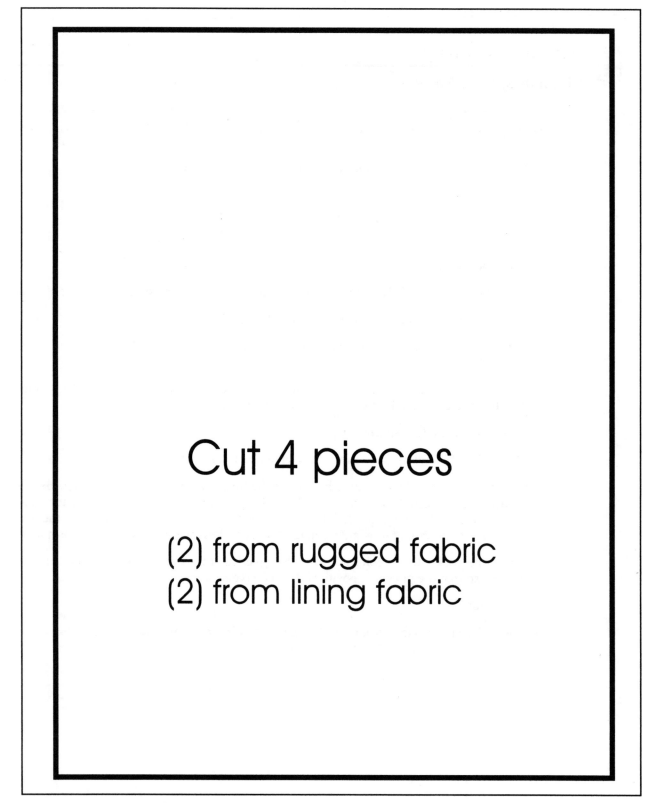

Fig. 7.2. Transplant pocket pattern.

From *Beyond the Bean Seed*. © 1996. Nancy Allen Jurenka and Rosanne J. Blass. Teacher Ideas Press. (800) 237-6124.

Treat

Transplanter's Punch

4 8-ounce cans of lemon-lime soft drink
1 small can of lemonade
1 32-ounce can of pineapple juice
a few drops of red food coloring

Serve in 8-ounce paper cups or glasses. Decorate with skewers that have been threaded with chunks of pineapple and maraschino cherries.

Poem

Symons, Arthur. "The Gardener." In *A Book of Nature Poems*, by William Cole. Viking, 1969.

Word Play

"I feel like a transplant" expresses that uneasy feeling of dislocation we feel when we've gone to a new camp, school, home, or group.

Read More About It

Hershey, Rebecca. *Ready. Set. Grow! A Kid's Guide to Gardening.* Goodyear, 1995. 104 pp. (P-I).

Hunt, Linda, Marianne Frase, and Doris Liebert. *Celebrate the Seasons.* Herald, 1983. pp. 54-56. (P-I).

Jordan, Helene J. *How a Seed Grows.* HarperCollins, 1992. 32 pp. (P).

LeTord, Bijou. *Rabbit Seeds.* Four Winds, 1984. 32 pp. (P).

Mintz, Lorelie. *Vegetables in Patches and Pots.* Farrar, Straus & Giroux, 1976. pp. 35-41. (I).

Sunset Editors. *Best Kids' Garden Book.* Sunset, 1992. pp. 25-27. (P-I).

Chapter 8
Gardening Gadgets

Gardeners love gadgets. They also love tinkering, experimenting, and being resourceful. That's what this unit is all about. The lessons are "Scarecrows," "Tunnels, Tents, and Tipis" "Problem Solvers," "Tools," and "Trash to Treasure."

Although some lessons are best done in Summer, such as the string bean tipis in "Tunnels, Tents, and Tipis," other activities may be done in the Winter or on a rainy day when it is too muddy and wet outside to garden. "Trash to Treasure" is a good example of a Winter or indoor lesson. These lessons will get kids thinking, problem solving, and being inventive. Encourage divergent thinking and creativity as you lead your boys and girls through these lessons.

8.1 Scarecrows

Littlewood, Valerie. *Scarecrow!* Dutton, 1992. 29 pp. (P-I).
Gardeners are always looking for ways to control pests, such as birds. Littlewood documents the devices and strategies employed by various cultures—British clappers, Japanese kakashi—in her attractively illustrated book in which she describes the history, lore, and crafts associated with scarecrows. Littlewood includes easy-to-follow directions for scarecrow construction.

Gardening Activity

Construct a Scarecrow

Have the children construct a scarecrow. Have on hand:

newspaper

old pants

pumpkin head or a stuffed pillowcase or
   burlap bag

shirt

two broom or mop handles or
   dowels

Have the boys and girls follow these directions:

1. Attach or make facial features on the object chosen to be the head. Stuff it if necessary.

2. Lash the broom handles together to create a cross or armature.

3. Attach the clothing to the armature. Stuff with the newspaper.

4. Attach the head.

Language Arts Activity

Let's Pretend

Present this pretend scenario to your group:
The scarecrows are all upset. They are being displaced by the Pesticides. They are going to lose their jobs.
Have the children write and present a one-act skit that shows:

- how the scarecrows reacted to the news
- what they decided to do about it
- how they went about getting it done
- what characters there will be
- who will play what role

Have them do a line, circle, or square dance at the end of the skit to celebrate.
Have your group listen to several musical pieces and then have them select the music for their dance. Two possibilities are:

"Turkey in the Straw"
"The Wabash Cannonball"

Square dance music may be obtained from:

Supreme Audio, Inc.
P.O. Box 50
Marlboro, NH 03455-0050
1-800-445-7398
   or
Wagon Wheel Records and Books
17191 Corbina Ln. # 203
Huntington Beach, CA 92649

As an alternative, read aloud "Six Crows: A Fable" by Leo Lionni. Have your group make up a skit based on this fable.

Creative Activity

Costumes

Have the students brainstorm about costuming "The Pesticides."

Have the boys and girls create the costumes for the skit. Straw hats, blue jeans, and checked shirts or similar attire should do.

Treat

Caramel Apple Scarecrows

7 apples	14-ounce bag of caramels
2 tsp. water	popsicle sticks
gum drops	licorice strings cut into 3" and 6" lengths
candy corn	construction paper

Prepare a device for holding the caramel apples while they are being decorated. One suggestion is a weighted egg carton. Fill an egg carton with sand and tape it shut. Set aside.

1. Prepare apples by washing them and inserting a popsicle stick into each.

2. With a dab of white glue, attach a cross piece (another popsicle stick) underneath the apple.

3. Melt caramels with water in a double boiler.

4. Dip the apples into the melted caramels. Place on waxed paper to firm up the caramel.

5. When the caramel feels tacky, insert the entire structure into the egg carton so you can decorate it.

6. Decorate the coated apple with licorice string hair and candy corn facial features.

7. Cut out a paper costume using the pattern provided (fig. 8.1 on page 109). Drape the paper costume over the cross arms. Secure with cellophane tape in the back or staple.

Poem

Franklin, Michael. "The Scarecrow." In *A Small Child's Book of Verse*, compiled by Pelagie Doane. Oxford, 1948.

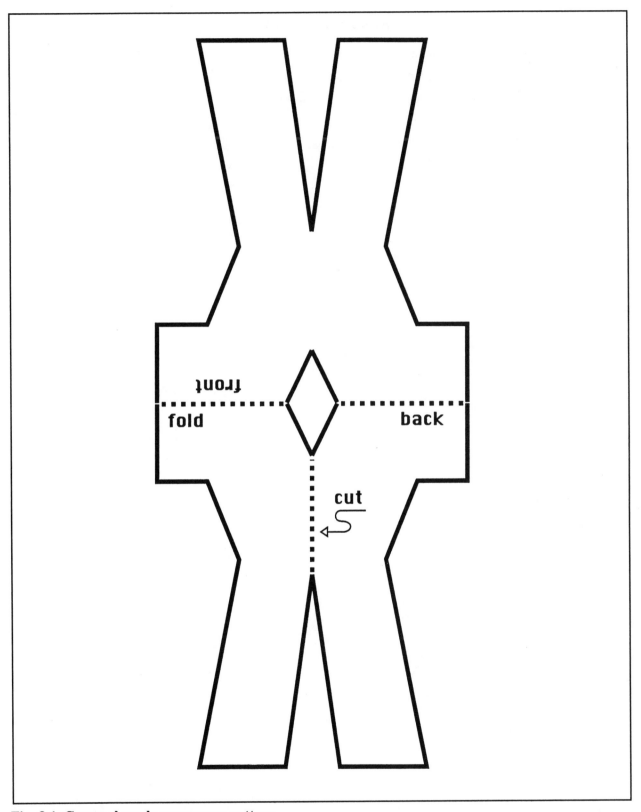

Fig. 8.1. Caramel apple scarecrow pattern.

Read More About It

Giblin, James, and Dale Ferguson. *Scarecrows.* Crown, 1980. 55 pp. (I).

Lionni, Leo. *Six Crows: A Fable.* Knopf, 1988. 32 pp. (P).

San Souci, Robert. *Feathertop.* Doubleday, 1992. 32 pp. (P-I).

Schertle, Alice. *Witch Hazel.* HarperCollins, 1991. 29 pp. (P-I).

Stolz, Mary. *The Scarecrows and Their Child.* Harper & Row, 1987. 67 pp. (I).

8.2 Tunnels, Tents, and Tipis

Markmann, Erika. "Your Little Corner of the World." In *Grow It! An Indoor/Outdoor Gardening Guide for Kids.* Random House, 1991. 47 pp. (P-I). Illustrated by Gisela Konemund.

For the city gardener Markmann's book gives good information about growing, caring for, and propagating indoor plants. She even provides good advice to boys and girls about how to care for their plants when they have gone on vacation. She encourages city children to garden outdoors on balconies, porches, and terraces. On pages 36 and 37 she shows children how to build a silver lace vine tent.

Gardening Activity

Hide-Aways

Along with the boys and girls, browse through children's garden books to get ideas for hide-aways. As a group, decide on one. Build a framework with your students using the directions from one of the books. Some of your choices may be a tunnel of PVC pipe and chicken wire, a tipi of bamboo poles, or a house frame of stakes.

Plant material to cover these frameworks may be red runner beans, silver lace vine, corn, sunflowers, morning glories, or gourds. Keep the center of these structures weed-free with a mulch of black plastic or straw or both.

Language Arts Activity

Uninterrupted Reading

After these structures are covered with plant material, have your children enjoy their favorite books in an uninterrupted manner by allowing them to read inside the structure.

Suggestions are:

Miss Penny and Mr. Grubbs by Lisa Ernst (P)

Rabbit Seeds by Bijou LeTord (P)

The Plant Sitter by Gene Zion (P)

Tom's Midnight Garden by Philippa Pearce (I)

The Secret Garden by Frances Burnett (I)

79 Squares by Malcolm Bosse (I)

Anna's Garden Songs by Mary Steele (P-I)

Creative Activity

3-D Construction

Have on hand:

marshmallows

gum drops (giant size and regular)

pretzel sticks

licorice ropes

peppermint canes and sticks

Distribute about eight marshmallows and a handful of pretzel sticks to each child. The other candy may be used as optional choices.

Instruct the students to construct any three-dimensional object they imagine with the pretzels and marshmallows. Don't overload them with how-to's; let their imagination and thinking skills take over.

Treat

Construction Treats

Eat the constructions made during the Creative Activity.

Poem

Roberts, Elizabeth Madox. "The Butterbean Tent." In *Sung Under the Silver Umbrella*, by The Literature Committee of the Association for Childhood Education. Macmillan, 1956.

Read More About It

Fell, Derek. *A Kid's First Book of Gardening*. Running Press, 1989. pp. 87-88. (I).

Kramer, Jack. *Plant Sculptures*. Morrow, 1978. 63 pp. (I).

Lovejoy, Sharon. *Hollyhock Days*. Interweave, 1994. pp.47; 53-64. (I).

———. *Sunflower Houses*. Interweave, 1991.144 pp. (I).

Paul, Aileen. *Kid's Outdoor Gardening*. Doubleday, 1978. 77 p.

Tilgner, Linda. *Let's Grow!* Storey Communications, 1988. pp. 72-74. (I).

8.3 Problem Solvers

Ocone, Lynn, with Eve Pranis. *National Gardening Association Guide to Kids' Gardening.* Wiley, 1990. 148 pp. (I).

One of the most authoritative books about children's gardening, this comprehensive text on school and community gardening will provide readers with everything they need to know about starting up and maintaining gardens. It not only covers basic gardening completely but also makes connections to other curricular areas, including science. Problems from working with city governments, to inventing handy devices, to preventing vandalism are addressed. *Guide to Kids' Gardening* is considered a bible for starting a school and community garden program for children.

Gardening Activity

Gardeners Are Problem Solvers

Successful gardeners are active problem solvers. They don't just throw up their hands and walk away when something goes wrong and something invariably goes wrong when gardening. This quality makes for a successful human being as well as a persevering gardener. Identify several problems you are having with your gardening project. Duplicate this problem-solving outline (fig. 8.2 on page 114) and use it to solve the problems.

State the problem: _____.

Restate it as a goal to be achieved. If that goal is too big for immediate solution, break it up into baby steps. Think of the advantages and disadvantages to each objective. Think of the outcome that will result for each objective.

EXAMPLE

Problem: Our garden is pretty but no one else sees it.

Goal: To attract visitors to our garden.

Objective: To bring younger children from the day care center to visit.

Advantages	Disadvantages	Outcome
Little kids will get to see what they can do when they get older.	They will need to be watched.	Little kids will learn about gardening.
Little kids like short trips.	They will need games. They will need to be taught.	We will get to show off our garden.

Problem-Solving Outline

Problem: _____

_____

_____

_____

Goal: _____

_____

_____

_____

Objective #1 _____

_____

Objective #2 _____

_____

_____

Advantages	Disadvantages	Outcome
_____	_____	_____
_____	_____	_____
_____	_____	_____
_____	_____	_____
_____	_____	_____
_____	_____	_____
_____	_____	_____

Fig. 8.2. Problem-solving outline.

Language Arts Activity

Ask Ms. or Mr. Gardener

Create a group newspaper. Have the boys and girls write all types of garden-related articles and have a column called "Ask Mr. (or Ms.) Gardener" or a more colorful, clever name. Have the boys and girls take turns being the answer person and being the ones generating the questions.

Or, depending on your situation, actually publish the newspaper and distribute it on a regular basis among people in your camp, synagogue, neighborhood, church, school, or set of families. Develop a clientele of real people who have real problems for your boys and girls to solve.

Creative Activity

Plastic—Problem or Problem Solvers?

Brainstorm. Have on hand plastic bleach bottles, quart-size soda bottles, gallon size water bottles. Get your boys and girls to generate a list of 20 items to create from plastic bottles.

Have your kids search back issues of *Growing Ideas* and other gardening newsletters and magazines for more ideas.

Make as many of your ideas as you can. Display them in a downtown store window or at your local shopping mall to encourage folks to recycle and to give them ideas.

Treat

Mystery Pie

Once upon a time, a baker had no apples to make a pie. To solve her problem, she invented the following recipe:

2 cups broken (not crushed) crackers	2 tsp. cream of tartar
2 cups water	2 Tbs. lemon juice
1 cup white sugar	1 Tbs. lemon zest
1/2 cup brown sugar	2 Tbs. butter
1/2 cup honey	1 tsp. cinnamon
Pastry for a two-crust pie	

Line a 9" pie plate with pastry. Place crackers in the lined pie plate.

In a saucepan put the water, sugars, honey, and cream of tartar. Bring to a boil over high heat. Turn down the heat and simmer this mixture for 15 minutes. Remove from heat. Stir in butter, lemon juice, zest, and cinnamon. Pour over crackers. Place pastry on top. Seal. Bake at 425° for 35 minutes. Cool before serving.

Word Play

"In a pickle" is a way some people say that they have a problem.

Read More About It

Ehlert, Lois. *Mole's Hill.* Harcourt Brace, 1994. 32 pp. (P).

Ernst, Lisa. *Miss Penny and Mr. Grubbs.* Macmillan, 1991. 32 pp. (P).

Keller, Beverly. *The Beetle Bush.* Coward, McCann & Geoghegan, 1976. 64 pp. (P).

Moore, Elaine. *Grandma's Garden.* Lothrop, Lee & Shepard, 1994. 32 pp. (P-I).

Wilkins, Verna, and Gill McClean. *Five Things to Find: A Story from Tunisia.* Tamarind, 1991. 24 pp. (P).

8.4 Tools

Tilgner, Linda. *Let's Grow!* Storey Communications, 1988. 208 pp. (I).

Readers are given 72 informative and fun gardening activities. Planting Native American gardens, making corn husk dolls and scarecrows, planting a fruit tree, growing mold gardens, making sunprints, and pressing flowers are just a few of the many lively activities described. The book supplies sound gardening advice and instructions. The black and white photographs of highly enthusiastic young gardeners motivate readers to try their hand at these projects.

Especially worth noting are the suggestions about working with very young children and children with disabilities, such as a physically disabled or developmentally delayed child.

Information about tools is given on pages 22-26.

Gardening Activity

Taking Care of Tools

A good gardener respects tools. He or she uses them safely and knows the function of each. Gather a bunch of rusty, muddy garden tools.

Assemble paint, salt, lemons, steel scouring balls (not steel wool), oily rags, and oil.

Have children clean up the tools and scour off the rust with a paste of salt and lemon juice. Paint the handles. Oil any joints and hinges that may be found on pruning tools.

Discuss the name of each tool and its function. Discuss the safety rules for each.

Language Arts Activity

Safety Rule Posters

Write a list of safety rules elicited from a discussion with the boys and girls. Have each child pick one of the rules to illustrate a safety poster. Keep it simple. Distribute books illustrated by Lois Ehlert. Distribute brightly colored paper, glue, and scissors.

Have the boys and girls create safety posters in the cut-paper graphics style of Lois Ehlert.

Creative Activity

Redesigning Tools

Discuss these statements and questions with your group:

There must be a better way; there must be a safer way; there must be another way.

How can a tool be improvised? Suppose you had no hoe. What could you use? Suppose you had no shovel. What would you use?

Suppose you had to carry a pile of dirt or straw or manure and had no wheelbarrow. What would you use?

How would you redesign a rake so that a person sitting in a wheelchair could use it?

How would you scare away mice?

How would you redesign a trowel so you could plant small plants in a bottle?

How would you redesign a hoe so blind gardeners could find it again after they put it down?

Have your group discuss the problems and fill in the redesigning tools chart (fig. 8.3 on page 118). Add other cells as necessary.

Tool Chart

Tool	Use	Change	New Function
Trowel	Dig in garden to transplant plants.	Make it very narrow.	Dig around rocks and crevices.
Long-handled shovel			

Any tool	Needs to be found after it's been laid down.	Make it more findable for:
		  a regular gardener
		  a blind gardener
		  a wheelchair gardener
			Found more easily.

Fig. 8.3. Tool chart.

Treat

Shovels

Do we ever use one food as a tool to handle another food?

Serve celery sticks with paper cups of dip.
1/2 pint sour cream
1 Tbs. tomato relish
1/4 cup green peppers chopped
1/4 cup red peppers chopped
dash of Worcestershire sauce
Watch your boys and girls shovel in this treat.

Poem

Flemming, Elizabeth. "My Barrow." In *The Golden Flute*, by Alice Hubbard. John Day, 1932.

Word Play

Tool words are used in everyday expressions:

He sure raked Mr. Morton over the coals.
She's got a hard row to hoe.
Jamie shoveled birthday cake into his mouth.

Read More About It

Fell, Derek. *A Kid's First Book of Gardening*. Running Press, 1989. pp. 17-18. (P-I).

Hunt, Linda, Marianne Frase, and Doris Liebert. *Celebrate the Seasons*. Herald Press, 1983. p. 22.

Kirkus, Virginia. *The First Book of Gardening*. Watts, 1956. 78 pp. (P-I).

Ocone, Lynn, with Eve Pranis. *National Gardening Association Guide to Kids' Gardening*. Wiley, 1990. pp. 20 and 90. (I).

Sunset Editors. *Best Kids Garden Book*. Sunset, 1992. pp. 10-11.

Waters, Marjorie. *The Victory Garden Kids' Book*. Globe Pequot, 1994. 148 pp. (I).

8.5 Trash to Treasure

Carlson, Laurie. *EcoArt*. Williamson, 1993. 157 pp. (P-I).
Chock-full of easy-to-follow directions for art and craft projects, *EcoArt* will lead your group toward creative uses for junk and throw-aways. Several sections are garden-related, so pick and choose among these projects, most of which take about 30 minutes to complete.

Gardening Activity

Trash to Treasure Garden

Look around your area. Find a small spot that is ugly and trash-filled. Ask the owner's permission to improve it. Do what is necessary to fix it up. It may be something simple, such as picking up the trash and pulling weeds, to something elaborate, such as planting a tree and small garden. Be sure to take before and after photographs. If you use black and white film with a glossy finish, your hometown newspaper is more likely to publish them. Given enough notice, your local news team may come out with a camera crew and put your kids on the evening news. Nothing like positive publicity to raise a child's self-esteem.

Language Arts Activity

Watch and Discuss *The Secret Garden*

Rags to riches, trash to treasure, garbage to compost are ways to show that something wonderful has come from something poor.
Read aloud *The Secret Garden* or watch it on videotape.
Discuss how this book/movie demonstrates the theme of transforming trash to treasure.

Creative Activity

The Resourceful Gardener

Inventiveness and resourcefulness are two qualities that many gardeners possess. Encourage the development of these qualities in your young gardeners by doing any of the activities related to gardening in *EcoArt*. Have the boys and girls bring in the same item so you have multiples of things that might be thrown out, such as egg cartons, shoe boxes, yogurt cartons, ice cream cartons, plastic mesh bags, or paper towel tubes.
Have a brainstorming session during which you generate a long list of highly divergent responses to the question "What could be make out of _____ ?"
Have your children choose an item to make from their throw-away. Find a public display case for them, perhaps at the shopping mall. Title the display appropriately, e.g., "Twenty Ways to Use Yogurt Cups."

Treat

Candied Orange Peel

Throw the orange rinds into the trash? Never! Turn that trash into treasured candied orange peel.

Prepare orange peel:

Slice oranges in half. Juice. Save juice. Clean out the inside of the orange. Cut the peel into strips. Place into a saucepan. Cover with water, set on the stove, and bring to a boil. Lower heat and simmer for 15 minutes. Drain. Scrape away the white part. Cut into very thin strips with scissors. Use the recipe below.

1 cup sugar
1/2 cup water
1 cup prepared orange peel

Bring the sugar and water to a boil. Add the orange peel. Cook until the peel is almost transparent. Remove the peel with a slotted spoon and spread out on a platter to cool. Roll in granulated sugar.

Poem

Jones, Brian. "The Garden of a London House." In *A Flock of Words*, ed. David Mackay. Harcourt Brace, 1969.

Read More About It

Brown, Marc. *Your First Garden Book*. Little, Brown, 1981. 48 pp. (P-I).

Kohl, Mary Ann, and Cindy Gainer. *Good Earth Art*. Bright Ring Press, 1991. 220 pp. (I).

Milord, Susan. *The Kids' Nature Book: 365 Indoor/Outdoor Activities and Experiences*. Williamson, 1989. 158 pp. (I).

Ocone, Lynn, with Eve Pranis. *National Gardening Association Guide to Kids' Gardening*. Wiley, 1990. pp. 74, 81, 82, 84, 89, and 100. (I).

Van Allsburg, Chris. *Just a Dream*. Houghton Mifflin, 1980. 48 pp. (P-I).

Chapter 9
Garden Inhabitants:
Friend or Foe?

Earthworms, insects, lizards, frogs, toads, and spiders are only a few garden inhabitants who may be friends or foes, pests or pals of plant life. Have your youngsters get acquainted with some garden inhabitants by experimenting with earthworms, collecting and studying available insects, keeping a Carolina anole as a pet, gathering and raising tadpoles, and collecting and spray painting spider webs. Have fun with riddles and tongue twisters; play "The Spider and the Fly Game" with your boys and girls. Have them collect and retell spider folktales, engage them in reader's theater or choral reading, solving a mystery, and making dioramas. Serve chameleon cooler and tarantula treats.

9.1 Earthworms

Appelhof, Mary. *Worms Eat Our Garbage: Classroom Activities for a Better Environment.* Flower Press, 1982. 232 pp. (I).

The more than 150 classroom activities, designed for fourth- through eighth-grade classrooms, inspire observational and problem solving explorations that are non-harmful to the worms being studied. Clever "wormformation" boxes contain nitty gritty biological background information. Investigative activities such as worm composting and worm food preferences show how plants respond to worm casting and help students understand important life science concepts.

Gardening Activity

Bean Plant Experiment

Have on hand two sets of three pots of bean plants (six total). In one set of three pots, place thirty (ten worms each) live red wigglers. Cover the red wigglers with some dampened soil. In the second set of pots place no red wigglers. Place the two sets of pots together and give equal amounts of light, water (don't overwater and drown the red wigglers) and diluted fertilizer. Compare and contrast the growth of the six bean plants over the growing season.

Language Arts Activity

Read Aloud and Perform

Read aloud *How to Eat Fried Worms* by Thomas Rockwell. With boys and girls rewrite, assign roles, rehearse, and perform as a readers' theater or choral reading.

Creative Activity

Raise and Sell Earthworms

Raising earthworms can be a profitable business for young people, retirees, small independent entrepreneurs, and large commercial growers. Search out and interview people in your community who raise earthworms for bait, fertilizer, or breeding stock. Raise and sell worms as a group project to subsidize gardening expenses.

Treat

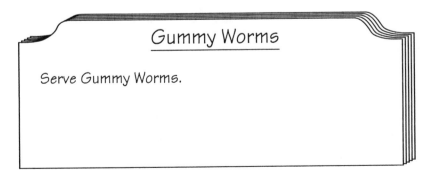

Gummy Worms

Serve Gummy Worms.

Poem

McEwen, Catherine Schaefer. "The Earthworm." In *Away We Go! 100 Poems for the Very Young.* Crowell, 1956.

Word Play

The scientific name for earthworms is *oligochaete*, which comes from two Greek words: *oligo*, meaning few, and *chaet*, meaning bristle. Oligochaete therefore means "few bristles."

Read More About It

Appelhof, Mary. *Worms Eat My Garbage.* Flower Press, 1982. 100 pp. (I).

Hess, Lilo. *The Amazing Earthworm.* Scribner, 1979. 48 pp. (I).

Kalman, Bobbie, and Janine Schaub. *Squirmy Wormy Composters.* Crabtree, 1992. 32 pp. (P-I).

McLaughlin, Molly. *Earthworms, Dirt, and Rotten Leaves.* Atheneum, 1986. 86 pp. (I).

Soutter-Perrot, Andrienne. *Earthworm.* Creative Edition, 1993. 32 pp. (P).

9.2 Insects: Pests or Pals?

Doris, Ellen. *Entomology*. Thames & Hudson, 1993. 64 pp. (I).
   Produced in association with The Children's School of Science in Wood's Hole, Massachusetts, the book explains how to study insects. The various insect orders are described and, where appropriate, instructions about how to raise them are provided. Caterpillars, crickets, and milkweed bugs are likely candidates for successful insect-raising projects. Insect habits and habitats are described. Biological supply houses are referenced at the end of the book for those who wish to raise and study insects.

Gardening Activity

Collect Insects

   Collect and study commonly available insects. Use a magnifying glass and/or a jeweler's loupe to examine body parts, i.e., the kind of head, the shape of body, the number of legs, the kind of wings. Visit a nearby nature museum to view its insect collection. Invite an entomologist to talk with boys and girls and tell them what an entomologist does.

Language Arts Activity

Read Aloud and Rewrite

   Read aloud the patterned picture book *The Outside Inn* by George Lyon. In this book a puddle and its contents are used by four children to offer the reader some "snacks." The simple rhyming text provides a model for creative writing. Have your group change the word "puddle" to "garden" and "waiter" to "gardener." Proceed to have them rewrite the text in an appropriate manner.
   In addition, read it aloud and have children respond as a chant. Most children will get a kick out of its silliness.

Creative Activity

Solve the Mystery

   Read aloud "Firefly and the Ape" from George Shannon's *Fifteen Folktales Around the World*. Tell boys and girls to listen carefully and to be prepared to solve the mystery.

Treat

Bugs on a Log

Cut celery sticks. Spread with peanut butter. Sprinkle with raisins.

Poem

Lear, Edward. "The Daddy Long Legs and the Fly." In *The Complete Book of Nonsense*. Castle Books, 1994.

Word Play

For riddles see *Bugs* by Nancy W. Parker and Joan R. Wright (Greenwillow, 1987).

Read More About It

Brinckloe, Julie. *Fireflies!* Aladdin, 1985. 32 pp. (P).

Fleming, Denise. *In the Tall Tall Grass.* Holt, 1991. 32 pp. (P).

Ganeri, Anita. *Insects.* Watts, 1992. 32 pp. (I).

Goor, Ron, and Nancy Goor. *Insect Metamorphosis: From Egg to Adult.* Atheneum, 1991. 32 pp. (P-I).

Lavies, Bianca. *Backyard Hunter: The Praying Mantis.* Dutton, 1990. 32 pp. (I).

Mound, Laurence. *Insect.* Knopf, 1990. 64 pp. (I).

Selsam, Millicent. *Where Do They Go? Insects in Winter.* Four Winds, 1982. 32 pp. (P-I).

Souza, D. M. *Insects in the Garden.* Carolrhoda, 1991. 40 pp. (P).

9.3 Lizards

Chase, G. Earl. *The World of Lizards*. Dodd, Mead, 1982. 144 pp. (I).
The author examines the physical characteristics and behavior of monitors, chameleons, iguanas, geckos, poisonous lizards, and others and relates anecdotes concerning his work as the curator of the Black Hills Reptile Gardens.

Gardening Activity

Pet Chameleon

The Carolina anole, also known as the American Chameleon, is found in the southeastern United States and makes a good pet, although it is not a true chameleon. The true chameleon is native to Africa and Asia and is difficult to keep as a pet.

To keep a pet American Chameleon you will need a large aquarium. Cover the bottom of the aquarium with clean gravel from a pet supply store. Add green plants and a mirror. Feed your chameleon one live mealy worm daily. Mist the aquarium with water daily to provide the chameleon with water for lapping.

Watch your chameleon for color changes. Color changes are due to light, temperature, emotions, and state of health. The Carolina anole will be brown during the day or when it's cold and will turn green at night or when it's warm. It will also turn green when it sees its image. Color changes may take as long as 10 minutes. Keep a log of the color changes that you observe.

Language Arts Activity

Write Couplets and Stories

Use Nancy Parker's *Frogs, Toads, Lizards, and Salamanders* as a model to write couplets and stories about lizards.

Creative Activity

Food Chain Web

Use what you have learned about lizards to develop a food chain web. See page 30 of Virginia Harrison's *Where Animals Live: The World of Lizards* for a model.

Treat

Chameleon Cooler

unsweetened, natural, purple grape juice
freshly squeezed lemon juice
sodium bicarbonate tablets—available from pharmacies

Purple grape juice will turn red by adding a small amount of freshly squeezed lemon juice. Add one sodium bicarbonate tablet to grape and lemon juice to change the color to the original purple and then to blue.

Poem

Buchanan, Ken, and Debby Buchanan. *Lizards on the Wall*. Harbinger House, 1992.

Word Play

The expression "leaping lizards" is sometimes said when someone is surprised. It was a favorite of Little Orphan Annie. Someone referred to as a "chameleon" has a changeable personality.

Read More About It

Harrison, Virginia. *The World of Lizards*. Gareth Stevens, 1988. 32 pp. (P-I).

Ivy, Bill. *Our Wildlife World: Lizards*. Grolier, 1990. 28 pp. (P-I).

Parker, Nancy Winslow, and Joan Richards Wright. *Frogs, Toads, Lizards, and Salamanders*. Greenwillow, 1990. 48 pp. (P-I).

Schnieper, Claudia. *Chameleons*. Carolrhoda, 1989. 47 pp. (P-I).

Smith, Trevor. *Amazing Lizards*. Knopf, 1990. 29 pp. (P-I).

9.4 Frogs and Toads: The First Voices on Earth

Lobel, Arnold. *Frog and Toad Together*. Harper & Row, 1971. 63 pp. (P).

Use this beloved classic as a springboard to the study of frogs and toads. Chapters are self-contained stories that can be read independent of the others. The second chapter, "The Garden," features Toad as the impatient gardener waiting for his seeds to grow. Children already familiar with Frog and Toad might enjoy Beatrix Potter's, *Mr. Jeremy Fisher*. Older children may prefer Samuel Clemens's story "The Celebrated Jumping Frog of Calaveras County."

Gardening Activity

Raise Tadpoles

Gather and raise tadpoles in an aquarium. Early Summer is the best time to collect tadpoles from a pond. Collect only a few. With a pail or nets scoop them up. Gather pond water and a few water plants from the pond to add to your aquarium. Let the water stand for 24 hours before adding tadpoles. Change the water frequently. Be sure to always let the water stand overnight before adding it to the aquarium. You can feed your tadpoles fish food. Don't overfeed. Release your tadpoles back into their home pond after you have finished observing them for several weeks.

Language Arts Activity

Observe and Record Changes

Observe and keep a log of the changes that occur in your tadpoles. Record your care of the tadpoles; that is, what and when you fed them and when you changed the water. Draw pictures and make a chart of how tadpoles become frogs.

Creative Activity

Shoebox Diorama

Amphibians such as frogs and toads were the first creatures to emerge from their watery homes and inhabit the earth. Frogs and toads are sometimes called "the first voices on earth." Using what you have learned about frogs and toads, i.e., their food and life-sustaining environment, what do you suppose their early world was like? What plant and animal life existed in the water and on earth? Research and prepare a shoebox diorama.

Treat

Gummy Frogs

Serve Gummy Frogs.

Poem

Posey, Anita E. "The Bullfrog's Song." In *A Child's First Book of Poems*. Western Publishing, 1981.

Word Play

For riddles, cartoons, silly stories, and tongue twisters see *Un-Frog-Gettable Riddles* by Joanne E. Bernstein and Paul Cohen (Whitman, 1981); *The Yellow Brick Toad: Funny Frog Cartoons, Riddles, and Silly Stories* by Mike Thaler (Doubleday, 1978); or *Fast Freddie Frog and Other Tongue Twister Rhymes* by Ennis Rees (Boyds Mills, 1993).

Read More About It

Clarke, Barry. *Amazing Frogs and Toads*. Knopf, 1990. 29 pp. (P-I).

Gibbons, Gail. *Frogs*. Holiday House, 1993. 32 pp. (P-I).

Lee, Jeanne M. *Toad Is the Uncle of Heaven: A Vietnamese Folk Tale*. Holt, 1985. 32 pp. (I).

Parker, Nancy Winslow, and Joan Richards Wright. *Frogs, Toads, Lizards, and Salamanders*. Greenwillow, 1990. 48 pp. (P-I).

Thaler, Mike. *The Yellow Brick Toad: Funny Frog Cartoons, Riddles, and Silly Stories*. Doubleday, 1978. 96 pp. (P-I).

Wiesner, David. *Tuesday*. Clarion, 1991. 32 pp. (P-I).

9.5 Spiders

Ryder, Joanne. *The Spiders Dance*. Harper,1981. 40 pp. (P-I). Illustrated by Robert Blake.

Ryder's poetry tells the story of a spider's life. Blake's illustrations of blue, yellow, and green portray baby spiders emerging from their nest. Soon these weave webs, trap food, grow, mate, and lay their own eggs. This charming book is sure to engage the interest of children across age levels. After reading this book, boys and girls may be interested in learning that the tarantella dance was named after the tarantula. *The Spiders Dance* would make a good nonfiction companion to *Charlotte's Web*.

Gardening Activity

Spider Webs

Before starting this activity, research spider books to identify poisonous spiders in your area, such as the black widow or brown recluse spider. Know what the webs of the black widow looks like and avoid them for this activity. Read these directions to your group:

Different kinds of spiders spin different kinds of webs. The four main types of webs are funnel, sheet, maze, and orb webs. Look for and photograph different kinds of spider webs. Collect webs by using a can of spray paint and stiff a piece of paper or cardboard. Use light-colored paint with dark paper, or dark-colored paint with light paper. Spray a web lightly from both sides. Press the paper against the web so the web adheres to the paper. Cut around the web. Label and display your webs on bulletin boards. Draw pictures of the spiders that make each kind of web and display these with the webs.

Language Arts Activity

Collect and Retell Spider Folktales

Explore the spider in myths, folklore, and even superstitions around the world. Boys and girls may already be familiar with the well-loved classic *Charlotte's Web*, the Greek myth about Arachne, and the African tales about Anansi. Begin with *Someone Saw a Spider: Spider Facts and Folktales* by Shirley Climo. Collect and retell spider folktales. Compile your own book of spider facts and superstitions. Use the opportunity to differentiate between fact and superstition.

Creative Activity

The Spider and the Fly

This is a game often played at various nature centers or camps:

String a spider web path about waist high. Blindfold one player who will be the spider. Other players will be flies. Each fly will quietly find a place in the web.

The spider will place a hand on the web and follow the web to find a fly.

Call time after one minute.

When the spider finds a fly, the fly will become the next spider and the spider will become a fly.

Treat

Tarantulas

V-shaped roasting rack
4 dried, pitted prunes
bright orange gum drops

16 tubular licorice twists
4 Tbs. of peanut
butter

Drape licorice twists over the roasting rack so they form an M shape. Place in oven for about 15 minutes at lowest temperature (about 200°) until licorice twists are limp and look like an M. Remove. Let cool and harden.

Cut prunes open, remove pit, and cut two small slits near one end (eye sockets to be used later). Stuff each prune with approximately 1 tablespoon of peanut butter.

Arrange 4 licorice M's as legs and hold them up while placing prune, peanut-butter-side down, at the middle of the M's. The peanut butter will hold legs together.

Cut small triangles of orange gum drops for eyes and insert into the eye sockets previously cut in the prune.

Makes 4 servings.

Boys and girls might be interested in knowing that licorice comes from the roots of the licorice plant, which is a member of the legume family.

Poem

Collymore, Frank. "The Spider." In *Peeling the Onion: Anthology of Poems*, ed. Ruth Gordon. HarperCollins, 1993.

Word Play

"As creepy as a spider" is a common simile.

Read More About It

Climo, Shirley. *Someone Saw a Spider: Spider Facts and Folktales*. Crowell, 1985. 133 pp. (I).

Hopf, Alice L. *Spiders*. Cobblehill, 1990. 64 pp. (P-I).

Kimmel, Eric. *Anansi and the Giant Melon*. Holiday House, 1994. 32 pp. Illustrated by Janet Stevens. (P-I).

Lovejoy, Sharon. "Spiders, Please Stay." In *Hollyhock Days*. Interweave, 1994. pp. 81-82. (I).

McNulty, Faith. *The Lady and the Spider*. Harper, 1986. 44 pp. (P).

Parsons, Alexandra. *Amazing Spiders*. Knopf, 1990. 29 pp. (P-I).

Roth, Susan L. *The Story of Light*. Morrow, 1990. 32 pp. (P-I).

Chapter 10
Garden Habitats

Design and plant habitats intended to attract such garden inhabitants as butterflies, birds, bees, small animals, or an array of wildlife. Habitats intended to attract butterflies, birds, or bees may be a plot of ground, a windowsill, or a container garden. For small animals or an array of wildlife select a plot of ground.

You may wish to begin by visiting similar habitats in your community. Ask the librarian or media generalist at your public or school library or at your local arboretum, garden center, or botanical or zoological gardens for assistance in collecting print and nonprint reference materials and in developing the basic reference skills of your boys and girls. Visit local nurseries to see and select plants. To develop your plot of ground, request assistance from your Cooperative Extension Service, Master Gardeners, Federated Garden Clubs, or gardening members of your community.

10.1 Butterfly Habitats

Sedenko, Jerry. *The Butterfly Garden*. Villard, 1991. 144 pp. (I).
The author shares his love of butterflies and gardens in this informative resource book augmented by full-color photos. The preface includes history, folklore, and even poetry. Sedenko describes the life cycle of butterflies and provides a guide to butterflies, flowers, and plants with suggestions and designs for the butterfly garden. Finally, he includes appendices listing plants by mail, butterfly gardens to visit, butterfly organizations, native plant organizations, and suggestions for further reading.

Gardening Activity

Design and Plant

Design and plant gardens intended to attract butterflies. Your butterfly garden may be a plot of ground, a windowsill, or a container garden. Select a variety of plants for continuous bloom that will appeal to a variety of butterflies, such as lantana for monarchs, coreopsis for fritillaries, and lilies for tiger swallowtails. If your garden is a plot of ground, include the butterfly bush, which attracts butterflies like no other plant.

Language Arts Activity

Read Aloud

Read aloud "The Butterfly That Stamped" by Rudyard Kipling.

Creative Activity

Egg Carton Caterpillars

Materials:

    egg carton bottoms

    pipe cleaners

    magic markers

    scissors

    tempera paint

    brushes

Cut the egg carton in half lengthwise. Punch two holes on the top of one end, about 1/2 inch apart. Insert pipe cleaner through the holes to make feelers. Use magic markers or tempera paint to draw the eyes and then color your caterpillar.

Treat

Nectar

Suck sweet clover or honeysuckle to sample butter-fly nectar. Be sure to gather from an unsprayed area away from the road.

Poem

Roscoe, William. "The Butterfly's Ball." In *All Creatures Great and Small*, by Isabelle Brent. Little, Brown, 1994.

Word Play

"Butterflies in the stomach" is a common simile.

Read More About It

Carle, Eric. *The Very Hungry Caterpillar.* Philomel, 1987. 16 pp. (P).

Feltwell, John. *Butterflies and Moths.* Dorling Kindersley, 1993. 61 pp. (P-I).

Florian, Douglas. *Discovering Butterflies.* Aladdin, 1990. 32 pp. (P).

French, Vivian Caterpillar. *Caterpillar.* Candlewick, 1993. 24 pp. (P-I).

Herberman, Ethan. *The Great Butterfly Hunt: The Mystery of the Migrating Monarchs.* Simon & Schuster, 1990. 48 pp. (I).

Lovejoy, Sharon. "A Caterpillar Cave." In *Hollyhock Days.* Interweave, 1994. pp. 58-61. (I).

Ryder, Joanne. *Where Butterflies Grow.* Dutton, 1989. 32 pp. (P). Illustrated by Lynne Cherry.

10.2 Bird Habitats

Ehlert, Lois. *Feathers For Lunch*. Harcourt Brace Jovanovich, 1990. 32 pp. (P-I).

Readers are introduced to both garden plants and birds. Illustrations and rhyming text identify 12 common birds, their calls, and the environments in which they may be found. Both birds and plants are labelled. The storyline is held together by the adventures of a stalking cat that is attempting to catch one of those birds. A glossary at the end of the book gives pictures and information about the size, diet, home, and geographic area of each bird. Although written for primary-age children, this book will appeal to older boys and girls and serve as an introduction to identifying birds and designing gardens that will attract birds. Bold, colorful illustrations lend themselves to follow-up activities using collage and labels.

Gardening Activity

Design and Plant Bird Gardens

Design and plant gardens intended to attract birds. You may choose to attract a variety of birds, or limit yourself to a specific bird such as the hummingbird. Read Christine Widman's *The Hummingbird Garden* and plant bee balm, columbine, phlox, and other flowers blooming in the hummingbird lady's garden. Your bird garden may be a plot of ground, a windowsill, or a container garden. Hummingbirds and butterflies are attracted to many of the same flowers. If your garden is a plot of ground and you wish to attract hummingbirds, be sure to plant a trumpet vine.

Language Arts Activity

Create a Glossary

Using *Feathers for Lunch* as a model, identify birds in your geographic area and create a glossary that gives information about the size, diet, and home of each bird. Extend the activity by studying the migratory patterns of birds.

Creative Activity

Torn Paper Collage

Using *Feathers for Lunch* as a model, depict the birds in your area using torn construction paper collage. Label each bird and add to your glossary.

Extend the activity by exploring the significance of birds such as the legendary phoenix and thunderbird or the raven, crow, and owl in literature and art. The phoenix had its origin in Egyptian culture, whereas the thunderbird, raven, and owl figure prominently in Native American story, myth, and symbolism. Edgar Allan Poe's "The Raven" lends itself to choral reading. Adults may find Leonard Lutuack's *Birds in Literature* to be a richly informative resource.

Treat

Berries or Seeds

Sample some of the berries or seeds that birds like to eat. Blackberries, raspberries, strawberries, berry jam, or sunflower seeds are likely to be readily available choices.

Poem

Yolen, Jane. *Bird Watch*. Philomel, 1990. Illustrated by Ted Lewin.

Word Play

Birdwatchers like to use mnemonic devices to identify and remember bird calls. For example, they claim that the phoebe bird says its name, "phoe-bee," while the towhee sings out, "Drink your tea."

Read More About It

Climo, Shirley. *King of the Birds*. Crowell, 1988. 32 pp. (P). Illustrated by Ruth Heller.

Graham, Ada. *Six Little Chickadees: A Scientist and Her Work with Birds*. Four Winds, 1982. 56 pp. (I).

Parnall, Peter. *The Daywatchers*. Macmillan, 1985. 127 pp. (I).

Ryder, Joanne. *Dancers in the Garden*. Sierra Club, 1992. 32 pp. (P). Illustrated by Judith Lopez.

Yolen, Jane. *Bird Watch*. Philomel, 1991. 48 pp. (P-I). Illustrated by Ted Lewin.

10.3 Bee Habitats

Dowden, Anne Ophelia. *The Clover and the Bee: A Book of Pollination.* Crowell, 1990. 96 pp. (I).

The pollination partnership between plants and animals is examined for the budding horticulturist or the inquisitive naturalist. Insects, birds, mammals, wind and water as pollinators, and plant structure are discussed.

Gardening Activity

Pollination

Gather an assortment of flowers so that each child has one.

Identify the parts of the flower such as petal, stamen, pistil, and sepal. Examine the pistil. Have boys and girls touch the pollen with their fingers to see what happens. The pollen, which is usually yellow or orange, will stick to their fingers. Discuss how pollination occurs when pollen is carried from one flower to another by bees, insects, people, or the wind.

Language Arts Activity

Research and Report

Like ants, honeybees are social creatures who live in communities with specific jobs clearly assigned. Queen, drone, and worker bees cooperate and communicate to build and maintain their hives. Research the social life of honeybees. Report your findings by developing a diagram or chart showing life within a beehive.

Creative Activity

Busy Beezzzzz Paperweights

Materials:

> smooth oval rock, one for each child
>
> black, white, and yellow poster or tempera paint
>
> toothpicks
>
> tissue paper
>
> pipe cleaners
>
> glue

Directions: Paint smooth, oval rocks with yellow paint. Use black and white paint for eyes. Paint black stripes around the body after the yellow paint is dry. Glue part of a toothpick in place for a stinger. Bend a pipe cleaner into the shape of an 8 for wings. Glue tissue paper to the wing shapes. Trim when dry. Slightly bend the wings and glue to the body. Use as a shelf decoration or a paperweight.

Treat

Honey Tasting

Have a honey-tasting party by sampling various kinds of honey made from different blossoms.

Poem

Fisher, Aileen. "Bumblebee." In *Out in the Dark and Daylight*. Harper & Row, 1980.

Word Play

See *Busy Buzzing Bumblebees and Other Tongue Twisters* by Alvin Schwartz for tongue twisters about a bumblebee, a snake, a horsefly, a spider, a cricket, a bug, and a buttterfly.

Read More About It

Fischer-Nagel, Heiderose, and Andreas Fischer-Nagel. *Life of the Honeybee*. Carolrhoda, 1986. 46 pp. (I).

Hogan, Paula Z. *The Honeybee*. Raintree, 1979. 32 pp. (P).

Kelsey, Elin. *Nature's Children: Bees*. Grolier, 1985. 47 pp. (P-I).

Kerby, Mona. *Friendly Bees, Ferocious Bees*. Watts, 1987. 96 pp. (I).

Pringle, Laurence. *Killer Bees*. Morrow, 1990. 56 pp. (I).

10.4 Small Animal Habitats

Albert, Richard E. *Alejandro's Gift*. Chronicle, 1994. 32 pp. (P-I).

Alejandro, an old man living alone in the desert with his burro, discovers ways to attract animal visitors to his place. He discovers that when he plants a garden, he feels less lonely because of the small animals that come to visit. When he creates a waterhole that attracts desert animals, he has lots of company. A glossary with pictures of animals and birds of the Southwest appears at the end.

Gardening Activity

Exploration

Explore your garden, your neighborhood, or your community for small animals. What small animals do you find? Where do you find them? What do we mean by "habitat"? How can you create a habitat for small animals?

Language Arts Activity

Write Stories

Use *In My Garden* as a guide and model. Make up and write stories to go with pictures.

Creative Activity

Superstitions

Superstitions abound about small animals. What are superstitions? Gather your own collection about small animals. Use Thomas G. Aylesworth's *Animal Superstitions* and other references as resources.

Treat

Animal Crackers

Serve animal crackers.

Poem

Pomerantz, Charlotte. "Where Do These Words Come From?" In *Sing a Song of Popcorn,* by Beatrice Schenk de Regniers, Eva Moore, Mary Michaels White, and Jan Carr. Scholastic, 1988.

Read More About It

Cousins, Lucy. *Garden Animals*. Tambourine, 1991. (P).

Cristini, Ermanno, and Luigi Puricelli. *In My Garden*. Scholastic, 1981. 28 pp. (P).

Kuhn, Dwight. *More Than Just a Vegetable Garden*. Silver Press, 1990. 40 pp. (P).

Potter, Beatrix. *The Complete Tales of Beatrix Potter*. Warne, 1989. 383 pp. (P).

Schwartz, David. *The Hidden Life of a Meadow*. Crown, 1988. 40 pp. (P-I).

Wadsworth, Olive. *Over in the Meadow*. Puffin, 1985. 31 pp. (P). Illustrated by Mary Maki Rae.

10.5 Wildlife Habitats

Perenyi, Constance. *Growing Wild*. Beyond Words Press, 1991. 39 pp. (I).

Using paper-cutout illustrations, Perenyi tells how a lawn evolved from a clipped and perfect suburban lawn to a wild and weedy wildlife refuge. After the story is told, projects follow with lists of resources and organizations that support the notion of turning yards into refuges for birds and insects.

Gardening Activity

Wildlife Refuge

Do you have a refuge for wildlife in your garden, neighborhood, or community? How can you create one? What wildlife do you wish to attract: birds, bees, butterflies, small animals?

Language Arts Activity

Wildlife Notebook

Observe wildlife in your yard, your neighborhood, or a specific place in your community. Record your observations in your wildlife notebook.

Creative Activity

Edible Wildlife

Create edible wildlife creatures using marshmallows, raisins, toothpicks, and lots of imagination. Pinch, stretch, or cut marshmallows to create desired shapes.

Treat

Field Daisy Cupcakes

chocolate frosted cupcakes
marshmallows
yellow gumdrops
green gumdrop spearmint leaves

Decorate chocolate-frosted cupcakes with field daisies. Snip top half of marshmallows into six sections, cutting about 3/4 way through the marshmallows. Spread sections gently, pinching to resemble petals. Arrange them on top of frosted cupcakes. Place small yellow gumdrop in the center of each marshmallow. Place gumdrop spearmint leaves at the side of each flower.

Poem

Dickinson, Emily. "To Make a Prairie." In *Favorite Poems for Children*, by Holly Pell McConnaugly. Barnes & Noble, 1993.

Read More About It

Albert, Richard. *Alejandro's Gift*. Chronicle, 1994. 32 pp. (I).

Hunken, Jorie. *Botany for All Ages*. Globe Pequot, 1993. 184 pp. (I-Adult).

Johnson, Kipchak. *Worm's Eye View: Make Your Own Wildlife Refuge*. Millbrook, 1991. 40 pp. (I).

Katz, Adrienne. *Naturewatch: Exploring Nature with Your Children*. Addison-Wesley, 1986. 128 pp. (I).

Norsgaard, E. Jaediker. *Nature's Great Balancing Act: In Our Own Backyard*. Cobblehill, 1990. 63 pp. (I).

Wilkes, Angela. *My First Green Book*. Knopf, 1991. 48 pp. (P-I).

Chapter 11
City Gardening

Approximately 50 million children live in our cities. They need our most special, focused attention. Too often gardening is overlooked as an activity for city kids. Yet they are the very ones who may need the miracles and regeneration of spirit that nurturing a garden can often provide.

This chapter contains a variety of projects designed with the needs and opportunities of the urban child gardener in mind. Gardening in containers, in small places, in opportune places, and on balconies of apartment buildings is emphasized. Community outreach and the dissemination of information about gardening are encouraged.

Adult leaders working with gardens in the city have additional concerns that rural or suburban leaders may not have. In addition to considering soil and water conditions, city garden leaders will need to incorporate some civics lessons into the instructional mix. City gardening calls for cooperation among people and governmental agencies in order to establish community gardens. This is addressed in the last lesson of this unit, "Community Gardens."

11.1 Container Gardening

Bjork, Christina, and Lena Anderson. *Linnea's Windowsill Garden.* Raben & Sjorgren, 1978. 52 pp. (P-I).

Linnea is a city gardener with lots of advice and pointers for fellow city boys and girls. With the help of her friend, Mr. Bloom, a retired gardener, Linnea shows readers how to grow various indoor plants, how plants grow, how to water plants, how to get rid of pests, and how to tell when a house plant needs repotting. She even gives her readers directions for a game of chance to play when they tire of gardening.

Gardening Activity

Container Gardens

Have your boys and girls bring in an assortment of large items that could hold soil: garbage cans, waste-paper containers, buckets, barrel halves, plastic garbage bags, planters, window boxes, old tires.

Have them fill their containers with a potting mix (commercial or one of their own making). Have them decide what kind of garden they would like to plant in their containers by browsing through an assortment of books that cover container gardening.

Suggest the following types of gardens: miniature vegetables, thematic, salad, herbal, floral, one that focuses on a special color, or the very pragmatic kind that includes "whatever is available." Help them collect the seeds, seedlings, cuttings, or bulbs that they will need.

Language Arts Activity

Potted Poems

The structure of a poem could be thought of as its container. Cinquain is a type of poem with well-defined structure. Have your children follow these guidelines to produce each cinquain:

Cinquain is a five-line form that has a specific number of syllables per line.

Line Number	Number of Syllables	Example
Line 1	2	Our home
Line 2	4	Planted for us,
Line 3	6	Our sunflower houses
Line 4	8	Shelter us with yellow tiles as
Line 5	2	We read.

After your children have written their cinquain poems, bind them in a shape book cut to look like a classic clay pot.

Creative Activity

Oddest Container Contest

Succulents, such as hens and chicks, are able to grow under hostile conditions. They aren't prissy about their containers. They'll grow almost anywhere. Have a contest or have a display of the oddest container in which a succulent will grow. Suggestions are old toys, tennis shoes, an odd kitchen container, a dilapidated suitcase, an old lunch box, or a hub cap.

Have the members of your group search their surroundings for odd containers and have them plant succulents in them. Take care not to overwater.

Names of succulents include living stone, burro's tail, Mexican firecracker, and others as descriptive. Most are sedums or echevarias.

Treat

Edible Containers

Bake or buy small, round loaves of bread or hard rolls, just the right size for a small individual serving. Fill these with any thick hot soup or stew. Serve.

Poem

Greenaway, Kate. "Five Little Marigolds." In *V Is for Verses*, by Odille Ousley. Ginn, 1964.

Read More About It

Bjork, Christina, and Lena Anderson. *Linnea's Almanac*. Raben & Sjorgren, 1989. 60 pp. (P-I).

Bunting, Eve. *Flower Garden*. Harcourt Brace, 1994. 32 pp. (P).

Fenten, D. X. *Plants for Pots*. Lippincott, 1969. 128 pp. (I).

Markmann, Erika. *Grow It!* Random House, 1991. 47 pp. (I).

Walters, Jennie. *Gardening with Peter Rabbit*. Warne, 1992. 46 pp. (P-I).

Wilkes, Angela. *My First Garden Book*. Knopf, 1992. 48 pp. (P-I).

11.2 Yardstick Gardens

Waters, Marjorie. *The Victory Garden Kid's Book*. Globe Pequot, 1994. 148 pp. (I).

Young gardeners and their adult assistants are portrayed demonstrating good gardening practices. Readers find out how to begin, to plan, to dig, to purchase seeds, to plant, and to care for a child's garden. It's all here. This is an excellent basic book. A special feature of this book is the "Yardstick Garden." In every chapter Waters provides information about constructing and caring for a 3'-x-3' garden that is planned step by step for beginning gardeners.

Gardening Activity

Yardstick Gardens

Along with your group of boys and girls follow the directions for creating a yardstick garden given in the book.

Select a site 36" x 36" or fence in an area (could be a lawn or playground or blacktop) with concrete blocks. Fill it with soil and amendments. Afterwards, discuss what to plant. The book suggests beans, green peppers, and zinnias. Plant the garden and have the children tend it throughout a growing season.

You may wish to plant a late Spring garden of leaf lettuce, radishes, and pansies if you are in a school setting and want to have a harvest before June. The pansies are best purchased as seedlings.

Depending on the size of your group, you may wish either to build more squares or divvy up gardening tasks throughout the growing season.

Language Arts Activity

A Yard of Words

Give each individual pair or triad a yard-long piece of adding machine tape. Within five minutes have them write as many garden-related words as they can think of.

The winners could get a yard of licorice as a reward. The runners-up (everyone else) could receive an inch.

Creative Activity

Yardstick Treasure Hunt and Stats

Materials:

Yardsticks or yard lengths of rope for each child

the treasure hunt chart (fig. 11.1 on page 152)

Read or post these directions:

How many plants, animals, and things can you find that are 36 inches in length? Search your gardens, homes, and neighborhoods to find such items. Record your search on the chart provided.

The Treasure Hunt Chart

Item	Animal, Plant, or Thing	Where Found

Fig. 11.1. Treasure hunt chart.

From *Beyond the Bean Seed*. © 1996. Nancy Allen Jurenka and Rosanne J. Blass. Teacher Ideas Press. (800) 237-6124.

After a week or so of searching, combine the individuals' records into a group report displayed as a chart or bar graph.

Ask:

How many different kinds of plants did we find that were a yard high? How many plants of a specific type did we find?

How many gardeners were 36" high?

How many gardening tools were a yard long?

What is the total number of gardening related items we found? What were they?

How many items did we find that were 36" deep?

How many items did we find that were 36" long?

How many items did we find that were 36" high?

How many non-gardening related items did we find?

Do you think that many things around us are a yard long, deep, or high?

Treat

Mt.Stuart Elementary School's Yard-Long Vegetarian Bars

2 packages frozen dough for crescent rolls
2 8-ounce packages cream cheese,
    softened
1 package dry ranch salad dressing

black olives, chopped
1/4 cup cheese, shredded
3/4 cup Miracle Whip salad dressing

On a greased cookie sheet arrange the dough in two bars 20" by 3". Bake in a 375° oven for 10 minutes. Cool.

Mix cream cheese and dry ranch salad dressing with Miracle Whip salad dressing.

Arrange the two crusts on aluminum foil. Spread the seasoned cream cheese mixture over the crusts. Sprinkle on top 1 cup of a chopped vegetable mixture of all or some of the following:

red onions
green peppers
carrots
cauliflower

celery
mushrooms
broccoli

Add a sprinkling of chopped black olives and shredded cheese. Refrigerate for at least two hours.

Before serving, arrange on a serving board so that one 36" bar is formed. Sprinkle with fresh parsley or cilantro before serving.

Poem

Fisher, Aileen. "Counting Petals." In *Cricket in a Thicket*. Scribner's, 1963.

Read More About It

Lottridge, Celia Barker. *One Watermelon Seed*. Oxford, 1986. 24 pp. (P).

Lovejoy, Sharon. "A Floral Clock Garden." In *Sunflower Houses*. Interweave, 1991. pp. 32-40. (I).

Paul, Aileen. *Kids Outdoor Gardening*. Doubleday, 1978. 80 pp. (P-I).

Skelsey, Alice, and Gloria Huckaby. *Growing Up Green*. Workman, 1973. pp. 109-126. (I).

Stevenson, Peter, and Mike Stevenson. *Farming in Boxes: One Way to Get Started Growing Things*. Scribner's, 1976. 64 pp. (I).

Woolfit, Gabrielle. *Sow and Grow*. Thompson Learning, 1994. 32 pp. (P-I).

11.3 Improvised Gardens

Brown, Marc. *Your First Garden Book*. Little, Brown, 1981. 48 pp. (P-I).
Popular illustrator Marc Brown turns his artistic energy to sharing with children his love of gardening. This love and his humor come shining through each colorful page. Jam-packed with ideas, this book will inspire children and adults to garden and create. Plant-related projects, especially ones that use recycled products, include milk carton bird feeder, popsicle stick labels, and old shoe planters. Do you think gardening is for country kids? Marc gives a new/old definition to "crack" when he urges city kids to plant Crack Gardens by sprinkling alyssum, portulaca, and morning glory seeds into the cracks of neighborhood sidewalks. He puts a special emphasis on gardening ideas for city children. A list of sources and an index conclude the book.

Gardening Activity

Odd-Spot Gardens

Where is the oddest place you can find to plant a few seeds? Where could your children practice random acts of beauty? What drab place in your neighborhood could use a tiny touch of floral beauty or a patch of clover?

Take a walk with your boys and girls around your city neighborhood or someone else's neighborhood if you live in the country.

Find that odd spot that could use a sunflower, a scattering of poppies, or a bit of portulaca.

With seeds and some fertilized soil in hand, walk about scattering soil and seed.

Language Arts Activity

Placemat Maxims

Prepare 12"-x-18" drawing paper by setting off a 4"-x-6" space to be left blank. These spaces will later be filled with words of advice. Pass out the 12"-x-18" paper and crayons. Have your boys and girls draw in the outside border Marc-Brown-type cats going about the city planting seeds and plants in odd places.

Distribute 4"-x-6" pieces of paper. Have your children write advice to the rest of us about making the city prettier. Use this sentence starter:

"If you want to make our city prettier, . . ."

Paste these in the space set aside for it. Have the drawings laminated for placemats. Ask a local restaurant if they would like to use them.

Creative Activity

Garden Improv Theater

Have on hand a collection of hats, nylon netting, scarves, crepe paper, and costume paraphernalia. Give each group of four to six children a scenario to act out. Tell them to discuss their plans for their skits and to rehearse it.

Allow about 20 minutes for preparation and then have the performances. Don't make heavy weather over this activity; it's very informal.

Here are some suggestions for scenarios:

Bill Jones and Mary Smith are competing to see who has the biggest pumpkin. The judges come to visit each garden. All of a sudden . . .

Mr. Bear gardens all by himself. He is lonely. One day he looks up from his weeding. All of a sudden . . .

Captain Rose, Mrs. Rose, and their children Flora, Ruggie, and Mini grow a garden on a river barge. One day on their way down the river all of a sudden . . .

Treat

Yogurt Swirls

Swirl chilled orange juice and vanilla yogurt and some ice cubes together in a blender for a pick-me-up.

Poem

Davies, Mary Carolyn. "Gardening Is Heaps of Fun." In *V Is for Verses*, by Odille Ousley. Ginn, 1964.

Read More About It

Barrett, Judith. *Old MacDonald Had an Apartment House*. Atheneum, 1969. 32 pp. (P-I).

Dowden, Anne Ophelia. *Wild Green Things in the City*. Crowell, 1972. 56 pp. (I).

Perenyi, Constance. *Growing Wild*. Beyond Words, 1991. 39 pp. (P-I).

Rahn, Joan. *Nature in the City*. Garrard, 1978. 64 pp. (P-I).

Wilkes, Angela. *Growing Things*. Usborne, 1984. 24 pp. (P).

11.4 Porch, Patio, and Balcony

Muller, Gerda. *The Garden in the City*. Dutton, 1992. 40 pp. (P-I).
Originally published in Germany, this book shows readers how Caroline and Ben planted and cared for their backyard gardens in the city. They get help from Luke, a physically disabled child who gardens on a balcony above their backyard. The story unfolds as the seasons pass. Craft directions and recipes are woven into the seams of the narrative.

Gardening Activity

Share a Garden; Pass on a Legacy

Two main activities occur in this lesson: 1) a porch, patio, or balcony will be made more attractive with plants; 2) your children will get another group started with gardening. The first gets accomplished while doing the second.

Locate a porch, balcony, or patio that could be made more attractive with plants. Talk things over with the owner. Ask him or her if your boys and girls, along with another group, could design and create a container garden for their porch, patio, or balcony. Ask the owner if it is all right to take pictures and to use this project as publicity.

At the same time locate some other group (a preschool, a church group, a local family, a Brownie or a Cub Scout group, what have you) to use as learners and helpers with this community outreach project. Motivate and support this group to become gardeners while your children work with them to improve the appearance of the porch, patio, or balcony. One major way you are going to do this is by gathering gardening materials. If the gardening materials are available, the children of the second group will use them. Your boys and girls will act as the facilitators.

Have them gather the following items:

cardboard cartons (the kind that duplicating paper comes in are great)

potting soil mixes (perhaps ones that your group created)

seeds (perhaps gathered from your group's garden)

clean used pots, hanging baskets

starts of geraniums, coleus, spider plants, pothos

used garden-related books

how-to directions written by your group (content depends on your situation)

Have your children decorate the box. Have them title it "Garden Secrets in a Box." On the inside of the box lid have them print this message: "Gardening Brings Happiness; Pass It On!"

Pack the box and deliver it to the new group with a bit of ceremony. After all, your boys and girls are passing on the gardening legacy to others. That's cause for an event of note.

Over a period of several weeks have your group of children teach this new group how to propagate and care for indoor and outdoor container plants. When everything has been potted and the seeds or bulbs have sprouted, take the two groups of children and the potted plants to their new location, the porch, balcony, or patio chosen in the above section.

Assign the new group of gardeners the task of maintaining the porch garden with the owner's permission. This maintenance may consist of watering, fertilizing, pest control, and repotting plants to a larger container.

Over time take your group back to visit to see how the new gardeners are doing with their porch, patio, or balcony garden project. Help the new group prepare a new gardener's box ready to pass on soil, plants, containers, and instruction for another group. Naturally, you will want them to pass along the same admonition—find yet another group to pass the gardening legacy to and so on and so on until your city is filled with groups of gardening children willing and able to keep spreading the joy.

Language Arts Activity

Press Releases

Such a community outreach project as this gardening assistance one deserves some publicity for your group. Have your boys and girls write up a press release for your local newspaper. Be certain that they have included the who (with all the names spelled correctly), what, where, when, how, how much, and how many of good newspaper reporting. Be sure that the publicity release contains the theme: "Garden Secrets in a Box: Gardening Brings Happiness; Pass It On."

Actually submit this item to your neighborhood or local town newspaper so folks come to know what terrific gardening youngsters they have in their community.

Creative Activity

Before and After Photos

Get out the camera. Before, during, and after photographs of the gardening outreach project are in order. Display the photos with captions written by your group on a bulletin board that can be seen by the public.

Treat

Longwood Gardens Snow Creams

When the project is complete, a celebration is called for. When the folks at Longwood Gardens near Philadelphia celebrate, they like to serve this recipe:

2 envelopes unflavored gelatin
1/3 cup cold water
1 cup powdered sugar
1 1/2 cups heavy cream

1 pint sour cream
2 8-ounce packages
   cream cheese, softened

Soften the gelatin in the water and set aside.

Heat the heavy cream until it just begins to boil. Remove from heat. Add the sugar. Mix until the sugar is dissolved. Set aside.

Beat the cream cheese and the sour cream until it has no lumps.

Add the dissolved gelatin to the heavy cream. Beat until smooth to be certain there are no lumps.

Mix all the mixtures together. Pour into dessert glasses and chill. Serve with fresh fruit. Red raspberries are traditional.

Poem

Field, Rachel. "The Flower Cart Man." In *Sing a Song of Seasons*, by Sara and John Brewton. Macmillan, 1968.

Read More About It

Brown, Marc. *Your First Garden Book*. Little, Brown, 1981. 48 pp. (P-I).

Bunting, Eve. *The Flower Garden*. Harcourt Brace, 1994. 32 pp. (P).

Markmann, Erika. *Grow It*. Random House, 1991. 47 pp. (P-I).

Schaefer, Carole Lexa. *In the Children's Garden*. Holt, 1994. 32 pp. (P).

Skelsky, Alice, and Gloria Huckaby. "Baskets, Barrels, Bags." In *Growing Up Green*. Workman, 1973. pp. 127-131. (I).

11.5 Community Gardens

Huff, Barbara A. *Greening the City Streets*. Clarion, 1990. 61 pp. (I). Photographs by Peter Ziebel.

Full descriptions of community gardens are provided. Huff makes clear the values and advantages to society inherent in community gardens. Stories are told of how the people involved with community gardens solved the problems associated with them. Particularly encouraging are the stories of how community gardening enthusiasts triumphed over developers and dealt with bureaucracies.

Garden Activity

Start a Community Garden

Now that you and your group have your own garden and a good handle on gardening know-how, spread your enthusiam and expertise out into your neighborhoods or the next township. Start a community garden. Find a group of people who would like to help you and your group of young gardeners do this.

People who will want to help you and your children can be found among the children's parents and their friends; in churches, scouts groups, and Cooperative Extension programs; and among school personnel, urban green gorillas, and other community-oriented volunteers. So start asking around for help. Find out who else in your neighborhood is interested in starting a community garden. Write an article for the local paper telling what you want to do and ask for volunteers to meet at a certain place and time to have a start-up discussion.

Once you have assembled the volunteers, the children, and their parents together, you will need to have a discussion to consider such questions as the following:

Where can we have a community garden?

How do we get permission to use the land?

Where is the water source?

How much sunlight will it get?

How do we prevent vandalism and theft?

How can we get the soil prepared?

Who can help us obtain plants and seeds?

Where can we obtain tools? Shall we provide our own?

Do we need raised beds?

How do we keep weeding to a minimum?

Who will help us in case we need it?

Who is going to be responsible for doing what by what date?

How do we ensure that we keep the children involved and important within the project?

What kind of a timeline do we need?

Do we need funds raised? How?

Are we going to need insurance?

What other questions do we need to be asking and answering?

Resources for such a project can be found through:

The National Gardening Association
180 Flynn St.
Burlington, VT 05401
   or
American Community Garden Association
325 Walnut St.
Philadelphia, PA 19106

Get to a starting point with this steering committee. Set up subcommittees. Establish goals, objectives, and deadlines. Do it!

Language Arts

Public Relations Campaign

Such a project needs a variety of public relations pieces, such as announcements, posters, press releases, explanations, and brochures.

In addition, you may find the need to write letters asking for permission, for money, or for donations. Have your boys and girls write these persuasive pieces.

Talk with your children about the keys to successful persuasive writing: a request clearly stated and supported by logical reasons, an opinion backed by facts, writing that is appropriate to the reader, and answers given to arguments that the reader (the person you are trying to persuade or convince) may have.

Creative Activity

Thanking Volunteers

It is said of volunteers that they need to be thanked seven times in seven different ways. Brainstorm with your boys and girls as to how they might express their appreciation to all the volunteers who helped make the community garden a success. Here are seven to get you started:

   a thank-you note

   a thank-you tussie mussie (a Victorian nosegay)

   a thank-you mural

   an ad in the newspaper

   a thank-you button

   a thank-you tea

   a thank-you in a speech

Have your boys and girls thank their volunteer helpers.

Treat

Volunteers Chocolate Zucchini

All those volunteers need a party when the ground is first broken for the community garden. Here's what the people at the Chicago Botanic Garden like to serve to children and volunteers.

3 squares unsweetened chocolate
1 1/2 tsp. baking powder
1 tsp. salt
4 eggs
1 1/2 cups salad oil

3 cups unsifted flour
1 1/2 tsp. baking soda
3 cups sugar
3 cups grated zucchini
1 cup finely chopped nuts

Melt chocolate. Cool. Preheat oven to 350°. Grease and flour a 10-inch tube or bundt pan. Sift flour, baking powder, and salt. Set aside. In a large bowl, beat eggs until thick, then add sugar slowly. Beat well. Add salad oil and melted chocolate. Blend well. Add dry ingredients. Mix until smooth. Add grated zucchini and nuts. Mix well.

Pour batter into the prepared pan and bake 1 hour and 15 minutes. Cool in pan on wire rack. Sprinkle with powdered sugar. Serve.

Poem

Thompson, Blanche Jennings. "Ellis Park." In *Silver Pennies*, by Helen Hoyt. Macmillan, 1925.

Read More About It

Cutler, Katherine. *The Beginning Gardener.* Barrow, 1961. 173 pp. (I).

Disalvo-Ryan, Dyanne. *City Green.* Morrow, 1994. 32 pp. (P).

Dunks, Thom, and Patty Dunks. *Gardening with Children.* Harvest Press, 1976. 175 pp. (I-Adult).

Ocone, Lynn, with Eve Pranis. *National Gardening Association Guide to Kids' Gardening.* Wiley, 1990. 148 pp. (I).

Quattlebaum, Mary. *Jackson Jones and the Puddle of Thorns.* Delacorte, 1994. 113 pp. (I).

Trimby, Elisa. *Mr. Plum's Paradise.* Lothrop, Lee & Shepard, 1976. 32 pp. (P).

Waters, Marjorie. *The Victory Garden Kids' Book.* Globe Pequot, 1994. 148 pp. (P-I).

Annotated Bibliography

Approximate grade levels are indicated in parentheses: P = Primary, K-3; P-I = Grades 2-4; I = Intermediate, Grades 4-6. Bold numbers refer to lessons. RMA numbers refer to "Read More About It" sections at the end of the lessons.

A

Albert, Richard E. *Alejandro's Gift*. Chronicle Books, 1994. 32 pp. (P-I). Illustrated by Sylvia Long. **10.4**; RMA 10.5.

Alejandro, an old man living alone in the desert with his burro, discovers ways to attract animal visitors to his place. He discovers that when he plants a garden, he feels less lonely and that when he creates a waterhole that attracts desert animals, he has lots of company. A glossary with pictures of animals and birds of the Southwest appears at the end. Use this book to introduce the desert ecosystem.

Aliki. *Corn Is Maize*. Harper, 1976. 34 pp. (P-I). RMA 4.5.

Corn, first grown by Central and South American people, is a versatile vegetable now enjoyed throughout the world. Aliki tells the story of corn's history, propagation, value, and uses. Her two-color illustrations echo corn's green and gold. At the book's end she gives directions for craft projects.

Appelhof, Mary. *Worms Eat My Garbage*. Flower Press, 1982. 100 pp. (I). RMA 7.2.

Appelhof persuasively encourages her readers to take up worm composting. She explains in clear detail the how-to of maintaining a worm farm in one's house. In this day and age of recycling we need to pay more attention to what Appelhof is telling us.

Appelhof, Mary. *Worms Eat Our Garbage: Classroom Activities for a Better Environment*. Flower Press, 1982. 232 pp. (I). **9.1.**

The text contains more than 150 activities designed for ages 7 through 12. Featured are observational and problem-solving explorations that are nonharmful to the worms being studied. Clever "wormformation" boxes contain nitty-gritty biological information. These, combined with the investigative activities about such topics as worm composting or worm food preferences, show how plants respond to worm castings and help children understand important life science concepts.

Arnosky, Jim. *Crinkleroot's Guide to Knowing the Trees*. Bradbury, 1992. 32 pp. (P). RMA 6.5.

This guide to trees helps young readers identify leaf shapes, pine needles, and pine cones. Arnosky includes a diagram of growth rings. Information about seedlings and trees is provided.

B

Balan, Bruce. *The Cherry Migration*. Green Tiger Press, 1988. 32 pp. (I). RMA 5.3.

Anthropomorphic maraschino cherries escape from the soda fountain jar and roll off on an adventurous journey with ambiguous results.

Bang, Molly. *The Grey Lady and the Strawberry Snatcher*. Four Winds Press, 1980. 48 pp. (P-I). RMA 5.4.

In this wordless book fantasy, a strange character, the strawberry snatcher, follows the grey lady, who has just purchased a fine basket of strawberries for her family, to her home in the swamp. At the last minute she eludes him and he finds his own berries to pick. Wordless books may be used with all ages, and this one will appeal to older children. Elicit storylines from the children if you are aiming to increase their literacy skills.

Barrett, Judith. *Old MacDonald Had an Apartment House*. Atheneum, 1969. 32 pp. (P). RMA 11.3.

In this zany story, Mr. and Mrs. MacDonald become farmers within the confines of their apartment, much to the consternation of the neighbors and the landlord, Mr. Wrental.

Bash, Barbara. *Desert Giant: The World of the Saguaro Cactus*. Sierra Club Books, 1989. 32 pp. (P-I). RMA 6.3.

Illustrations of the southwest desert accompany an account of the life cycle and ecosystem of the saguaro cactus and the many forms of animal life it supports.

Beame, Rona. *Wildflowers: A Collector's Album*. Random House, 1994. 56 pp. (I). Illustrated by Dianne McElwain. **3.5.**

After opening this book tied shut with a pretty ribbon, readers are treated to watercolor paintings of wildflowers sorted by classes and the directions for collecting, pressing, and air drying them. Directions for mounting wildflowers within the book itself are given. Important to catch is the "Wildflower Collectors' Code." In the book the address for the National Wildflower Research Center is out of date. The address has been changed to 4801 LaCrosse Blvd., Austin, TX 78739. The last section instructs children how to create several craft projects from the wildflowers that they have collected. Beame and McElwain have created a beautiful book that children are likely to save for a lifetime once they have filled it with wildflowers.

Beck, Barbara L. *The First Book of Fruits.* Watts, 1976. 64 pp. (I). RMA 5.3.

The history, stories, and origins of major and rare fruits from all around the world are provided. Tie-ins with social studies are apparent.

Beskow, Elsa. *Peter in Blueberry Land.* Floris Books, 1987. (I). RMA 5.5.

While looking for berries for his mother's birthday, Peter meets the King of Berryland and his sons, who take Peter berry picking in this whimsical fantasy.

Bjork, Christina, and Lena Anderson. *Linnea's Almanac.* Raben & Sjorgren, 1989. 60 pp. (P-I). RMA 11.1.

Linnea, a self-professed city gardener, takes her young gardening fans through the year. She tells us what to look for and do month by month. Linnea includes birdwatching. Linnea loves headpieces; she tells us how to make dandelion garlands and leaf crowns. Teachers and youth leaders who are searching for ways to integrate reading with gardening may want to have children read the Linnea books to compare Linnea's experience with a helpful older gardener to Rosy's, the young gardener in Elizabeth Laird's *Rosy's Garden: A Child's Keepsake of Flowers.*

Bjork, Christina, and Lena Anderson. *Linnea's Windowsill Garden.* Raben & Sjorgren, 1978. 52 pp. (P-I). **11.1.**

Linnea is a young city gardener who has many helpful hints for her fellow city gardeners. With the help of her friend, Mr. Bloom, a retired gardener, Linnea shows readers how to grow various indoor plants, how plants grow, how to water plants, how to get rid of pests, and how to tell when a house plant needs to be repotted. She even gives her readers directions for a game of chance to play when they tire of gardening.

Bordewich, Fergus M. *Peach Blossom Spring.* Green Tiger, 1994. 42 pp. (P-I). Illustrated by Yang-Yi. RMA 5.2.

Delicate paintings in Chinese style lure the reader into the book and down the river to a magical, peaceful place found by a fisherman. The fisherman breaks his promise to the inhabitants when he tells others of this special place. When he returns, he cannot find it again.

Bourgeois, Paulette. *The Amazing Apple.* Addison-Wesley, 1990. 64 pp. (P-I). RMA 5.1.

This book includes lore, amazing facts, history, and recipes, as well as information about how apples grow and how they are cultivated and marketed. Bourgeois provides directions for making apple dolls and for putting on an Apple Party complete with games and treats.

Bourgeois, Paulette. *The Amazing Dirt Book.* Addison-Wesley, 1990. 80 pp. (P). RMA 7.1.

Can dirt be fun and educational? In the hands of Paulette Bourgeois it can. She has compiled two dozen fun projects for children. Throughout the book she has scattered amazing facts about soil and its properties.

Bremner, Elizabeth, and John Pusey. *Children's Gardens: A Field Guide for Teachers, Parents and Volunteers.* University of California Cooperative Extension Common Ground Garden Program, 1990. 186 pp. (I). RMA 7.3.

Bremner and Pusey have written a comprehensive text about gardening, especially about gardening with children in California. It is very well organized and the tabbed sections ease a searcher's task. The book covers site and soil preparation, plant choices, particularly for warmer parts of the United States, tools, pest management, starting seeds indoors, and transplanting.

Brenner, Fred, and May Garelick. *The Tremendous Tree Book.* Boyds Mills Press, 1992. 40 pp. (P-I). RMA 6.5.

This basic introduction to trees includes information on photosynthesis and unusual trees.

Brinckloe, Julie. *Fireflies!* Aladdin, 1985. 32 pp. (P). RMA 9.2.

Brinckloe's soft gray and yellow illustrations capture the feeling of a summer night when fireflies are flickering. She depicts a young boy's joy as he collects fireflies in a jar and then gives them their freedom.

Brown, Marc. *Your First Garden Book.* Little, Brown, 1981. 48 pp. (P-I) **11.3;** RMA 8.5, 11.4.

Jam-packed with ideas, this book will inspire children and the adults who garden with them to plant and create. Plant-related projects, especially ones that use recycled products, include milk carton bird feeders, popsicle stick labels, and old shoe planters. Do you think gardening is just for country kids? Brown has lots of ideas for city kids who want to plant. He gives a new/old definition to "crack" when he urges us to plant "Crack Gardens" by sprinkling alyssum, portulaca, and morning glory seeds into the cracks of neighborhood sidewalks.

Bruchac, Joseph. *The First Strawberries: A Cherokee Story.* Dial, 1993. 30 pp. (P-I). Illustrated by Anna Vojtech. **5.4.**

Storyteller and folklore researcher Joseph Bruchac brings this ancient Native American folktale to the attention of today's readers. In this story the first woman and first man quarrel. She storms off and the first man tries to catch up with her, but cannot. The sun causes strawberries to be strewn in the first woman's path. She picks them as a peace offering to the first man.

Bunting, Eve. *Flower Garden*. Harcourt Brace Jovanovich, 1994. 32 pp. (P-I). Illustrated by Kathryn Hewitt. **1.4;** RMA 11.1, 11.4.

Kathryn Hewitt's glowing illustrations and Bunting's rhyming text relate a contemporary urban story about a little girl and her father who plant a window box garden as a surprise birthday present for her mother. The title, therefore, may prove misleading to those looking for information about flower gardening with children, but *Flower Garden* is exquisitely ironic once the book has been read.

Burnie, David. *Flowers*. Dorling Kindersley, 1992. 61 pp. (P-I). RMA 3.1.

The cultivation requirements, habitats, and varieties of flowers are described by Burnie. He describes perfumed flowers, complicated flowers, and flowers that attract animals, to name a few. He classifies flowers by habitat, such as mountain, seashore, wetlands.

Burnie, David. *How Nature Works: 100 Ways Parents and Kids Can Share the Secrets of Nature.* Reader's Digest, 1991. 192 pp. (I). RMA 1.2, 6.1.

A complete life science course for children ages 8 to 12, this book is packed with easy-to-do experiments and activities that will help children discover how plants, animals, and systems work.

Burnie, David. *Plant*. Knopf, 1989. 64 pp. (P-I). **2.1;** RMA 2.2, 2.5.

Botany for the grade-school set. Plant parts are shown in clear, close-up photographs in the distinctive contemporary layout for which Eyewitness Books are known. The function of each plant part is explained with minimal text. Adaptation and habitats are described.

Busch, Phyllis. *Cactus in the Desert*. Crowell, 1979. 34 pp. (P). RMA 6.3.

Cactus life cycle and propagation are described in this book for primary-age children. Warm desert colors, mustard, ochre, terra-cotta, sage, and burnt sienna, match the subject matter. The relationship between cactus and water is emphasized.

Busch, Phyllis. *Wildflowers and the Stories Behind Their Names*. Scribner, 1977. 88 pp. (I). Illustrated by Anne Ophelia Dowden. RMA 3.5.

More than 60 wildflowers are described and illustrated. Lore, legends, and folktales about them are told. Dowden's illustrations make this a book to be valued.

C

Calhoun, Mary. *The Sweet Patootie Doll*. Morrow, 1957. 32 pp. (P-I). Illustrated by Roger Duvoisin. RMA 1.3.

Lucy made herself a doll from a sweet potato. She left the doll out on a stump, where a raccoon came upon her. A fox scared off the raccoon; then a bear came along and scared off the fox. A hound came by and scared off the bear. In spite of all these threats to her well-being, the sweet patootie doll survived. Librarians like to use this book for storytelling.

Campbell, Stu. *Let It Rot: The Gardener's Guide to Composting*. Storey Communications, 1990. 152 pp. (I). RMA 7.2.

For gardeners seeking the why, how, and what of composting, Campbell has written a comprehensive book on the topic. Campbell describes various methods of building compost piles and containers; he gives detailed directions for building bins. Campbell supplies long lists of specific items to put into a compost pile and the reasons to include them. For children who have a beginner's interest in chemistry, his explanations and charts concerning the chemical make-up of a compost pile are simple and informative. In addition to acquiring a working knowledge of an efficacious combination of nitrogen, phosphoric acid, and potash, readers will also discover the biological elements of a well-made compost pile. After reading this book and following Campbell's advice, the gardener will have gained riches in soil, crops, and knowledge.

Carle, Eric. *The Tiny Seed*. Picture Book Studio, 1987. 32 pp. (P). RMA 2.3.

The story of a seed and how it grows through the season is told and illustrated in Carle's distinctive style.

Carle, Eric. *The Very Hungry Caterpillar*. Philomel Books, 1987. 16 pp. (P). RMA 10.1.

A simple storyline is made splendid by Eric Carle's brilliantly colored illustrations. A caterpillar eats her way through a variety of fruits and vegetables before spinning a cocoon. An awesome butterfly is portrayed by Carle at the book's end.

Carlson, Laurie. *EcoArt*. Williamson, 1993. 157 pp. (P-I). **8.5;** RMA 1.5.

Chock-full of easy-to-follow directions for art and craft projects, *EcoArt* provides creative uses for junk and throw-aways. Several sections are garden-related. Laurie Carlson, an art teacher, describes dozens of projects to be constructed with an eye to nature and wise use of resources. Readers will find directions for making natural dyes, a portable easel, books, a cornhusk doll, mushroom spore prints, potpourri, rose petal beads, plastic jug projects, gourd bowls, and other treasures from trash.

Cavagnaro, David, and Maggie Cavagnaro. *The Pumpkin People*. Sierra Club Books, 1979. 32 pp. (P-I). RMA 4.2.

This photo-essay conveys the real-life story of a family who invited their friends to a harvest celebration. Everyone was encouraged to carve a jack-o'-lantern. At twilight a great collection of carved and lighted pumpkins was assembled and placed on scrapwood boats. This fantastic flotilla was launched and floated off into the sunset.

Chase, G. Earl. *The World of Lizards.* Dodd, Mead, 1982. 144 pp. (I). **9.3.**
The author examines the physical characteristics and behavior of monitors, chameleons, iguanas, geckos, and poisonous lizards. Chase relates anecdotes about his work as the curator of Black Hills Reptile Gardens.

Christensen, Bonnie. *An Edible Alphabet.* Dial, 1994. 32 pp. (P). RMA 3.4.
Children of many cultures are shown enjoying fruits, flowers, vegetables, and herbs. Christensen's wood engravings create a warm, cheerful alphabet book.

Clarke, Barry. *Amazing Frogs and Toads.* Knopf, 1990. 29 pp. (P-I). RMA 9.4.
Photographs illustrate the informative text about these amphibians.

Climo, Shirley. *King of the Birds.* Crowell, 1988. 32 pp. (P-I). Illustrated by Ruth Heller. RMA 10.2.
The author tells her version of one of the oldest and most universal legends, the one in which the birds choose a king. Long ago, Mother Owl devised a plan to end the quarreling of the birds. She decreed that whoever flew highest and longest should become king. Wren used his wits to win the contest, become King of the Birds, and establish peace in the bird kingdom.

Climo, Shirley. *Someone Saw a Spider: Spider Facts and Folktales.* Crowell, 1985. 133 pp. (I). RMA 9.5.
This collection of facts, myths, folklore, and superstitions about spiders from around the world concludes with explanatory notes and a bibliography of additional sources.

Cobb, Vicki. *Lots of Rot.* Lippincott, 1981. 35 pp. (P). RMA 7.2.
The author sends her readers out to explore mold and bacteria in order to understand how decomposition happens. The relationship of rotting to soil composition is explained.

Cole, Joanna. *The Magic School Bus Plants Seeds.* Scholastic, 1995. 32 pp. (P). Illustrated by Bruce Degan. **2.2;** RMA 2.3.
Miss Frizzle takes to the garden dressed in a garden-print dress. This time the school bus turns into a ladybug that travels down and around stamens, anthers, and pistils to show readers and Miss Frizzle's class pollination and seed production and dispersal.

Cousins, Lucy. *Flower in the Garden.* Candlewick, 1992. 8 pp. (P). RMA 3.1.
This board book introduces garden flowers to the toddler set.

Cousins, Lucy. *Garden Animals.* Tambourine, 1991. (P). RMA 10.4.
This board book introduces simple garden animals.

Cristini, Ermanno, and Luigi Puricelli. *In My Garden.* Scholastic, 1981. 28 pp. (P). RMA 10.4.
Cristini and Puricelli ask readers to find garden inhabitants.

Crowell, Robert. *The Lore and Legends of Flowers.* Putnam, 1982. 80 pp. (I). Illustrated by Anne Ophelia Dowden. RMA 3.2.
The stories of 10 beloved flowers (tulips, narcissus, crocus, iris, carnations, roses, nasturiums, dandelions, marigolds, and dahlias) have been collected and retold. Dowden's illustrations distinguish this book as a collector's item.

Cutler, Katherine. *The Beginning Gardener.* Barrow, 1961. 173 pp. (I). RMA 11.5.
Even though it is dated, Cutler's book has information that others do not, so it is worth your efforts to find it through interlibrary loan or to urge librarians to bring it out from archival status. Particularly useful are the lists of perennials and annuals in which these flowers are identified by color, thus helping the young landscape designer make decisions. For those interested in showing off, one chapter gives the procedures for putting on an exhibition.

Part Two tells how to create specialty gardens. The plans for creating bird, box, bulb, dish, friendship, herb, rock, seashore, terrarium, wildflower, and window gardens are described. In this day and age when youngsters and their adult leaders are searching for authentic ways to reach out to their communities, the chapter on setting up a Garden Information Center provides useful ideas.

D

Daddona, Mark. *Hoe, Hoe, Hoe! Watch My Garden Grow.* Addison-Wesley, 1980. 58 pp. (P). RMA 7.4.
Daddona has written a basic how-to gardening book for children. It covers how and where to site a garden, how to prepare the soil, and how to plant. Exclusively about vegetable gardening, it includes a section about starting vegetables from seeds indoors and how to transplant. Last frost date information is given, which is usually not found in other books.

Dean, Anabel. *Plants That Eat Insects: A Look at Carnivorous Plants.* Lerner, 1977. 32 pp. (I). RMA 6.4.

Black and white drawings augment a readable text that introduces a variety of insect-eating plants. The Venus's fly-trap, sundew, butterworts, bladderworts, fungi, and pitcher plants are described. The cobra plant, a pitcher plant that eats snakes and frogs as well as insects, is included. The story of these unusual wetland plants is likely to capture the interest of students.

Degan, Bruce. *Jamberry.* Harper, 1983. 32 pp. (P). RMA 5.4, 5.5.

Rollicking rhymes and fanciful illustrations portray a summer's day of berry picking by a young child and a lively bear.

DePaola, Tomie. *The Popcorn Book.* Holiday House, 1978. 32 pp. (P-I). RMA 4.5.

The life and times of popcorn are depicted in de Paola's distinguishable style. Popcorn has been a staple of the indigenous people of North and South America for centuries. The Iroquois shared it with the Pilgrims at the first Thanksgiving. Archeologists discovered popcorn in a bat cave in New Mexico and determined that it was 5,600 years old. This information, plus recent consumer research (Milwaukee and Minneapolis are the leading popcorn-consuming cities), is provided along with two recipes for popping corn.

Dietl, Ulla. *The Plant and Grow Project Book.* Sterling, 1993. 48 pp. (I). RMA 1.1, 1.3, 1.4, 2.4.

An indoor plant book, this work emphasizes plants that may be started from plant parts and seeds about to be thrown out. For example, the author urges children to save and plant date seeds and avocado pits. An added feature is the author's rating system of the difficulty of each project. Three green fingers mean that the plant may take a long time to root and patience will be called for.

Disalvo-Ryan, Dyanne. *City Green.* Morrow, 1994. 32 pp. (P). RMA 11.5.

Illustrated by Disalvo-Ryan, this story portrays what a little girl named Marcy, her adult friend Miss Rosa, and their neighbors can do to transform a vacant lot into a beautiful community garden. Gardening city children will find inspiration in this book. At the end of the book, directions are given for creating a community garden. The address for the American Community Garden Association is provided. A percentage of the proceeds of Disalvo-Ryan's book will be given to the ACGA.

Doris, Ellen. *Entomology.* Thames & Hudson, 1993. 64 pp. (I). Photographs by Len Rubenstein. **9.2.**

Produced in association with The Children's School of Science in Wood's Hole, Massachusetts, the book explains how to study insects. The author describes the various insect orders and, where appropriate, provides instruction about how to raise them, including directions on raising caterpillars, crickets, and milkweed bugs. Insect habits and habitats are described. A list of biological supply houses is given at the end of the book for those who wish to raise and study insects.

Dowden, Anne Ophelia. *The Blossom on the Bough.* Crowell, 1994. 71 pp. (I). RMA 2.5, 6.5.

Dowden explains the botanical facts about tree flowers, angiosperms, gymnosperms, and evergreens. She concludes with a description of the various forest regions of the United States.

Dowden, Anne Ophelia. *The Clover and the Bee: A Book of Pollination.* Crowell, 1990. 96 pp. (I). **10.3;** RMA 2.2.

The pollination partnership between plants and animals is examined. Dowden's study helps us appreciate the intricate relationship that has evolved between plants and bees over the centuries. She shows readers how plant shapes, such as saucer, bell, tube, and closed, attract different pollinators while protecting the nectar. In addition to the honeybee, Dowden discusses insects, birds, mammals, wind, and water as pollinators.

Dowden, Anne Ophelia. *From Flower to Fruit.* Ticknor & Fields, 1994. 56 pp. (I). RMA 2.2, 5.5.

"Flower's the name; fertilization's the game" might sum up Dowden's book in a jingle, but that would not do justice to her beautiful watercolors and the wealth of information in the text. Readers will discover the process of seed production and how many varieties of fruit exist. All is not what it seems: We learn that an almond is not a nut and that a burdock is a fruit.

Dowden, Anne Ophelia. *Wild Green Things in the City.* Crowell, 1972. 56 pp. (P-I). RMA 11.3.

For urban teachers seeking books to support a nature study unit, this is just the text. Common weeds found in empty lots, parks, and along railroad tracks are illustrated beautifully by Dowden.

Dunks, Thom, and Patty Dunks. *Gardening with Children.* Harvest Press, 1976. 175 pp. (I-Adult). RMA 11.5.

This book contains good ideas for the middle-grade student. In addition to the usual guidelines for gardening procedures, this book has a chapter on why gardening with children helps to develop an attitude of caring. It also contains a great (and rare) chapter on the history of school garden programs.

E

Eaton, Marge. *Flower Pressing.* Lerner, 1973. 32 pp. (P-I). RMA 3.1.

A how-to book about preserving flowers and plants by pressing them.

Eckstein, Joan, and Joyce Gleet. *Fun with Growing Things: A Guide to Indoor and Outdoor Gardening for Kids.* Avon, 1991. 135 pp. (P-I). RMA 1.4.

In addition to illustrated step-by-step instructions for growing plants indoors and out, this book includes such garden-related projects as drying flowers, leaf printing, and making a sponge garden.

Ehlert, Lois. *Feathers for Lunch.* Harcourt Brace Jovanovich, 1990. 32 pp. (P-I). **10.2.**

Children are introduced to both garden plants and birds. Illustrations and rhyming text identify 12 common birds, their calls, and the environments in which they may be found. Both birds and plants are labeled. The storyline is held together by the adventures of a stalking cat that is attempting to catch one of those birds. A glossary at the end of the book gives pictures and information about size, food, home, and geographic area of each bird. Although written for primary-school children, this book will appeal to older children as well and serve as an introduction to identifying birds and designing gardens that will attract birds. Bold, colorful illustrations lend themselves to follow-up activities using collages and labels.

Ehlert, Lois. *Growing Vegetable Soup.* Harcourt Brace Jovanovich, 1987. 32 pp. (P). **4.1.**

Visually exciting, this book gives the step-by-step process of growing 11 vegetables. A vegetable soup recipe for you to try with your students is on the back cover.

Ehlert, Lois. *Mole's Hill.* Harcourt Brace, 1994. 32 pp. (P). RMA 8.3.

Mole has a problem to solve. Fox, raccoon, and skunk want to build a path to the pond, and Mole's hole is in the way. What will mole do? Gardeners will be pleased with Mole's solution. Ehlert's artwork, inspired by Woodland Indian ribbon appliqué and sewn beadwork, creates a stunning visual effect. A beautiful tribute to her home state, Wisconsin.

Ehlert, Lois. *Red Leaf, Yellow Leaf.* Harcourt Brace Jovanovich, 1991. 32 pp. (P). RMA 6.5.

Would you like to know how to plant a tree? Lois Ehlert gives detailed directions for this activity at the end of her colorful book. In the text, which she has illustrated with collages, she tells how a sugar maple grows from seed to tree. In the process, she tells how the tree changes from season to season. Boerner Botanical Gardens in Milwaukee, Wisconsin, assisted with the technical detail. A bird treat recipe to hang on a tree is provided.

Ernst, Lisa. *Miss Penny and Mr. Grubbs.* Macmillan, 1991. 33 pp. (P). RMA 8.3.

Side by side, Miss Penny and Mr. Grubbs have been neighbors and gardeners for a long time. Mr. Grubbs wants to get one up on Miss Penny and pulls a mean trick on her, giving her quite a problem to solve.

Eyewitness Visual Dictionaries. *The Visual Dictionary of Plants.* Dorling Kindersley, 1992. 64 pp. (I). RMA 2.1, 2.5.

Illustrated are micrographs and cross sections of plants labeled with scientific names. Functions of plant parts as well as fundamental botanical processes, such as photosynthesis, pollination, and germination, are explained and illustrated.

F

Fell, Derek. *A Kid's First Book of Gardening.* Running Press, 1989. 96 pp. (I). RMA 4.3, 7.1, 7.3, 8.2, 8.4.

Directions for planning and tending the garden as well as descriptions of varieties of odd-colored and -sized vegetables are provided. The author also gives information about trees and shrubs.

Feltwell, John. *Butterflies and Moths.* Dorling Kindersley, 1993. 61 pp. (P-I). RMA 10.1.

Two-page-spread format provides basic information with photos.

Fenton, Carroll, and Herminie Kitchen. *Plants We Live On.* John Day, 1971. 128 pp. (I). RMA 2.5.

An updated version of a 1956 book titled *Plants That Feed Us,* this book describes the history, politics, geography, and families of food plants. Especially well covered is the section on foods contributed to our culture by Native American gardeners. The chapter on small grains traces the Middle Eastern origins of wheat and barley. A detailed explanation of the organization of plants into families precedes a series of chapters that describe in detail the food plant members of the various plant families. The reader finds out, for example, that asparagus, often referred to as a grass, is really a member of the lily family. Genetics, plant improvement, a history of agriculture, and the problems associated with feeding a large world population conclude the book.

Fenten, D. X. *Plants for Pots.* Lippincott, 1969. 128 pp. (I). RMA 1.1, 11.1.

In addition to explaining different ways to propagate plants, Fenten describes the care needed for 12 varieties of house plants. He urges his readers to focus on a new plant each month.

Fenton, Carroll Lane, and Herminie B. Kitchen. *Fruits We Eat.* John Day, 1961. 128 pp. (I). RMA 5.5.

The origin, cultivation, and commercial distribution of fruit are explained.

Fischer-Nagel, Heiderose, and Andreas Fischer-Nagel. *Life of the Honeybee.* Carolrhoda, 1986. 46 pp. (I). RMA 10.3.

Photos and text show how honeybees pollinate flowers and produce honey and beeswax.

Fleming, Denise. *In the Tall, Tall Grass.* Henry Holt, 1991. 32 pp. (P). RMA 9.2.

Fragmented text trails through the illustrations, giving the impression of insects hopping, gliding, and chomping their way through tall grass.

Florian, Douglas. *Discovering Butterflies.* Aladdin Books, 1990. 32 pp. (P). RMA 10.1.

This simple introduction to butterflies explains their life cycle.

Florian, Douglas. *Discovering Trees.* Aladdin Books, 1990. 32 pp. (P). RMA 6.5.

This book describes tree varieties, their life cycles, and their development.

Florian, Douglas. *Vegetable Garden.* Harcourt Brace Jovanovich, 1991. 32 pp. (P). RMA 4.1.

Illustrated by the author, this book relates in a very easy-to-read rhyme the story of a family planting, caring for, and harvesting their vegetable garden.

Ford, Miela. *Sunflower.* Greenwillow, 1995. 26 pp. Illustrations by Sally Noll. (P). RMA 3.3.

Just right for the emergent reader and gardener, this simply told story tells how a child grows a sunflower.

French, Vivian. *Caterpillar, Caterpillar.* Candlewick Press, 1993. 24 pp. (P-I). RMA 10.1.

This book, through the narration of the grandfather character, traces the evolution of a caterpillar from egg to butterfly.

Froman, Robert. *Mushrooms and Molds.* Crowell, 1972. 32 pp. (P). RMA 6.1.

Froman provides directions for experiments, basic information, and diagrams.

G

Ganeri, Anita. *Insects.* Watts, 1992. 32 pp. (I). RMA 9.2.

Covering basic entomology, Ganeri provides factual information about the types, characteristics, habits, and habitats of insects. Body parts and functions are described.

Ganeri, Anita. *Plants.* Watts, 1992. 32 pp. (I). Illustrated by Adrian Lascom. RMA 2.1.

The author covers basic botany: the what, why, how, and where of plants, plant parts, and plant types from algae to flowering plants. Includes many activities, such as making spore prints from mushrooms and creating terrariums. Also includes kid-pleasing amazing facts.

Gibbons, Gail. *Frogs.* Holiday House, 1993. 32 pp. (P-I). RMA 9.4.

This is a visually appealing book with a colorful format and labeled illustrations. It provides basic information about frogs, their life cycle, how they make sounds that mean different things, how they hibernate when it is cold, their place in the food chain, how they differ from toads, and their value to the garden.

Gibbons, Gail. *From Seed to Plant.* Holiday House, 1991. 32 pp. (P). RMA 2.2.

For the beginning reader Gibbons has written and illustrated an explanation of pollination and seed formation, distribution, and germination. Gibbons's clear drawings make botany comprehensible.

Giblin, James, and Dale Ferguson. *The Scarecrow Book.* Crown, 1980. 55 pp. (I). RMA 8.1.

A serious researcher, Giblin has turned his mind to scarecrows. He makes clear the multicultural connections possessed by this folk figure. The lore, history, and variety of scarecrows are told with lucid writing.

Gillis, Jennifer. *In a Pumpkin Shell.* Storey Communications, 1992. 58 pp. (P-I). RMA 4.2.

Pumpkin growers rejoice. Gillis's book gives you lots of creative uses for pumpkins and pumpkin parts. A good resource for teachers who want integrated curriculum ideas. Recipes included.

Glaser, Linda. *Tanya's Big Green Dream.* Macmillan, 1994. 47 pp. (I). **6.5.**

Tanya's Earth Day project last year was a bean seed experiment, but this year in fourth grade she wants to do something beyond a bean seed. She overcomes obstacle after obstacle to raise money to purchase a tree for the city park. Her classmates make her project their project, and all work as a team to achieve this goal.

Goldenberg, Janet. *Weird Things You Can Grow.* Random House, 1994. 48 pp. (P-I). Illustrated by Phoebe Gloeckner. RMA 3.3.

Cartoons! Comics! To appeal to your zany-minded gardener, offer this book filled with references to walking stick cabbages, string of beads, everlastings, and carnivorous plants.

Goor, Ron, and Nancy Goor. *Insect Metamorphosis: From Egg to Adult.* Atheneum, 1991. 32 pp. (P-I). RMA 9.2.
Photographs and text provide accurate information about the development of various types of insects.

Graham Ada. *Six Little Chickadees: A Scientist and Her Work with Birds.* Four Winds, 1982. 56 pp. (I). RMA 10.2.
This is an account of Cordelia Stanwood's bird life studies.

Guiberson, Brenda Z. *Cactus Hotel.* Henry Holt, 1991. 32 pp. (P-I). Illustrated by Megan Lloyd. RMA 6.3.
After a cactus seed is carried off by a pack rat and dropped under a palo verde tree, it sprouts and grows. Guiberson and Lloyd portray the story of a saguaro cactus and the desert animals that rely on it for survival. A story of desert interdependence.

H

Handelsman, Judith F. *Gardens from Garbage.* Millbrook, 1993. 48 pp. (P-I). **1.3.**
For librarians, classroom teachers, and youth leaders who want to begin gardening with children but who do not want to go full-out with a 10′-x-12′ summer-long garden, this may be just the book. Although it is written for children, adults will find plenty of ideas. Handelsman provides her readers with numerous clearly described projects that are simple, very affordable—she is talking about garbage, after all—and guaranteed to be successful. If you try out the pineapple-growing project, allow the top to dry out for a few days before planting it and keep in mind that it will take up to two years to produce another pineapple.
The sidebars contain plant vignettes. Did you know that workers building the pyramids in Egypt went on strike to obtain a ration of garlic? If you enjoy this kind of information, read also *Garden Sass* by Lucille McDonald (Thomas Nelson, 1971) for more.

Harmonious Technologies. *Backyard Composting.* Harmonious Press, 1992. 95 pp. (I). RMA 7.2.
Highly detailed, this book explains the intricacies of composting. It provides diagrams of several types of compost bins. Recipes for various types of layered compost are provided. An excellent resource list and bibliography are given. A particularly useful feature is the trouble-shooter's guide on page 91.

Harrison, Virginia. *The World of Lizards.* Gareth Stevens, 1988. 32 pp. (P-I). RMA 9.3.
Color photos and readable text introduce lizards and provide basic information. The manner in which information is presented lends itself to developing cause-and-effect relationships. A diagram of the food chain appears on page 30.

Hausherr, Rosmarie. *What Food Is This?* Scholastic, 1994. 40 pp. (P-I). RMA 2.5.
Cheerful, evocative photographs whet the reader's appetite to know more. Posing a question about a particular food on one page, Hausherr provides the answer on the next. She shows another way to classify plants and other foods and connects food to good nutrition. A book too good to miss, it belongs on every parent's bookshelf.

Heller, Ruth. *Plants That Never Bloom.* Sandcastle Books, 1984. 44 pp. (P-I). RMA 6.1, 6.2.
Mushrooms, seaweed, lichen, and ferns are illustrated in Heller's bold style and described in rhyming text.

Heller, Ruth. *The Reason for a Flower.* Grosset & Dunlap, 1983. 42 pp. (P). RMA 2.3.
With brilliant, warm-tone paintings and rhyming text, Heller explains why plants have flowers and how pollination occurs. Various seed types are illustrated, and an explanation about how seeds travel is given.

Herberman, Ethan. *The Great Butterfly Hunt: The Mystery of the Migrating Monarchs.* Simon & Schuster, 1990. 48 pp. (I). RMA 10.1.
A handsome account of monarch butterfly migration and how children and other nonscientist volunteers make significant contributions to scientific discovery.

Hershey, Rebecca. *Ready, Set, Grow! A Kid's Guide to Gardening.* Goodyear, 1995. 104 pp. (P-I). **7.4;** RMA 1.5, 2.4, 7.3, 7.5.
Divided into three parts, *Ready, Set, Grow!* tells children how to garden both indoors and outdoors. Acknowledging the current interest in connecting gardening with children's literature, Hershey includes a reading list with each of her activities. Craft activities and recipes are included in the third part.

Hess, Lilo. *The Amazing Earthworm.* Scribner, 1979. 48 pp. (I). RMA 9.1.
Text and black and white photographs depict the characteristics, habits, and beneficial effects of worms. Instructions on how to raise worms, how to train a worm to find its way through a maze, and other experiments are included.

Hitte, Kathryn, and William Hayes. *Mexicali Soup.* Parents Magazine Press, 1970. 38 pp. (P-I). Illustrated by Anne Rockwell. RMA 4.1.
Mama decides to play a trick on her family after receiving much advice about the making of her soup.

Hogan, Paula. *The Honeybee.* Raintree, 1979. 32 pp. (P). RMA 10.3.
Simple text and full-color illustrations tell the story of the honeybee.

Holmes, Anita. *Cactus: The All-American Plant*. Four Winds, 1982. 192 pp. (I). **6.3.**

The author shares her love for the desert and its many cacti by taking readers on a journey of discovery in this comprehensive resource. Graceful but detailed pencil drawings support the readable, informative text. The book describes the cactus's adaptation to and role in the natural environment as well as the distinguishing characteristics of various cacti. In addition, Holmes provides recipes for cooking and directions for raising cacti. Appendices include a map of North American desert areas and a listing of desert gardens, museums, and natural areas.

Holmes, Anita. *Flowers for You: Blooms for Every Month*. Bradbury, 1993. 48 pp. (I). **1.1.**

Christmas and orchid cacti are among the 12 potted plants chosen for 12 months of bloom. The introduction presents basic botany, such as plant parts, environmental needs, and instructions for caring for plants. A plant chart shows plants, their blooming seasons, and their environmental needs, such as light, temperature, and humidity.

Hopf, Alice. *Spiders*. Cobblehill, 1990. 64 pp. (I). RMA 9.5.

Informative text and brilliant photographs describe the shared characteristics and differences among a variety of interesting species of spiders found around the world. Webs, mating, motherhood, and spider ingenuity are discussed.

Huff, Barbara A. *Greening the City Streets*. Clarion, 1990. 61 pp. (I). Photographs by Peter Ziebel. **11.5.**

Full descriptions of community gardens are provided. Huff makes clear the values and advantages to society inherent in community gardens. Stories are told of how the people involved with community gardens solved the problems associated with them. Particularly encouraging are the stories of how community gardening enthusiasts triumphed over developers and dealt with bureaucracies.

Hunken, Jorie. *Botany for All Ages*. Globe Pequot, 1993. 184 pp. (I-Adult). RMA 2.1, 2.5, 10.5.

A complete botany course for the intermediate-grade set, the 9- to 13-year-olds. The activities get the children into their backyards, woods, meadows, parks, empty lots, and gardens to explore, observe, discover, ponder, ask questions, and communicate about nature. Plants and their parts and functions are objects of discovery lessons. Respect for and understanding of the interdependence of plants, animals, habitat, and humans are stressed. This is an excellent manual for youth leaders, parents, and teachers searching for a complete, informative, and fun nature study program.

Hunt, Linda, Marianne Frase, and Doris Liebert. *Celebrate the Seasons*. Herald Press, 1983. 163 pp. (P-I). RMA 7.5, 8.4.

Enchanting children's crayon drawings brighten an easy-to-follow text. Good gardening know-how for children is organized around the seasons. The section on planning is helpful. The recipes included whet children's appetites for vegetables. Follow the little ladybug and gather a batch of helpful hints.

I

Ikeda, Daisaku. *The Cherry Tree* . Knopf, 1992. 32 pp. (P). Illustrated by Brian Wildsmith.

Brian Wildsmith's jewel-tone illustrations enhance this beautiful story of hope and renewal. After World War II, Taichi and Yumiko help an old man care for a war-weakened cherry tree. Their care results in the cherry tree's blossoming once again, a sign to all that hope and care can offset the effects of destruction. Geraldine McCaughrean translated this story from Japanese and some libraries cataloged it under her name, rather than Ikeda's. Look for both.

Ivy, Bill. *Our Wildlife World: Lizards*. Grolier, 1990. 28 pp. (P-I). RMA 9.3.

Two-page-spread format with readable text and full-page color photos on opposite pages introduces a variety of lizards. Geckos, chameleons, skinks, whiptails, iguanas, monitors, wormed lizards, and horned toads are included with basic information about habitats, diet, mating, and self-defense. A short glossary appears at the end.

J

Jobb, Jamie. *My Garden Companion*. Sierra Club, 1977. 350 pp. (I). RMA 7.2.

A comprehensive treatment of gardening and its relationship to the environment, this book stresses an attitude of stewardship. It includes information about soil development, composting, recycling, developing new plants, siting the garden plot, and transplanting. It also tells young gardeners how to reach out to others through community gardens and helps them look ahead to career choices within horticulture.

Johnson, Hannah. *From Appleseed to Applesauce*. Lothrop, Lee & Shepard, 1977. 48 pp. (P-I). RMA 5.1.

Black and white photographs depict the life cycle, propagation, and varieties of apples. A recipe for applesauce ends the text.

Johnson, Hannah. *From Seed to Jack O'Lantern*. Lothrop, Lee & Shepard, 1974. 48 pp. (P-I). RMA 4.2.

Black and white photographs reveal the chronological story of pumpkins growing in a New Jersey pumpkin patch. A recipe for roasted pumpkin seeds is included.

Johnson, Kipchak. *Worm's Eye View: Make Your Own Wildlife Refuge.* Millbrook Press, 1991. 40 pp. (I). RMA 10.5.

This little book discusses ways to attract wildlife to the backyard and the role of wild plants and animals in ecology. The format encourages a discovery approach with introductory directions to "find out."

Johnson, Stephanie. *Tomatoes and Other Killer Vegetable Jokes and Riddles.* Doherty, 1992. 128 pp. (P-I). RMA 4.3.

Jokes and riddles will amuse readers.

Johnson, Sylvia. *Morning Glory.* Lerner, 1985. 48 pp. (I). Photographs by Yuko Sato. **3.3.**

The development of the morning glory from the planting of the seed to the dying of the withered vines and dispersal of new seeds is presented in extensive detail. Colored photos include labeled cross sections of the plant and seed. Of particular interest might be photos of the blossom, showing it begining to open at 3:00 AM and fully open by 4:00 AM. The book concludes with a one-page discussion of the morning glory family, which includes bindweed, dodder, and the vining sweet potato. A glossary of technical terms follows.

Johnson, Sylvia. *Mushrooms.* Lerner, 1982. 48 pp. (I). **6.1.**

Photographs, diagrams, and text provide information about some of the more than 38,000 different kinds of mushrooms. Mushrooms belong to the fungi family, a group of plants that do not make their own food. This book explains how mushrooms get their food, grow, and reproduce. It also relates which mushrooms are edible and which are poisonous. Scientific and common names are given. Of particular interest might be the explanation of mushroom fairy rings.

Johnson, Sylvia. *Potatoes.* Lerner, 1984. 48 pp. (I). Photographs by Masahuru Suzuki. RMA 4.4.

The cultivation of potatoes is explained in a scientific yet readable manner. Cross sections of dyed potatoes are shown to demonstrate the presence of starch. This book makes clear the difference between the fruit of a potato, which is not eaten, and the tuber, which is.

Jordan, Helene J. *How a Seed Grows.* HarperCollins, 1992. 32 pp. (P). Illustrated by Loretta Krupinski. RMA 2.3, 7.5.

Sweet pastel illustrations and a simple text tell the story of a little girl who explains how to plant bean seeds in an egg carton and how to transplant them after they have sprouted.

K

Kalman, Bobbie, and Janine Schaub. *Squirmy Wormy Composters.* Crabtree, 1992. 32 pp. (P-I). RMA 9.2.

Photographs of lively, enthusiastic, involved children tell the story of their introduction to vermi-composting. The care and feeding of red wigglers is explained so readers can start right in raising worms and learning the value of composting.

Katz, Adrienne. *Naturewatch: Exploring Nature with Your Children.* Addison-Wesley, 1986. 128 pp. (I). RMA 1.2, 10.5.

Written for both children and adults, this book tells the adults what to look for in meadows, seashores, woods, and gardens and how to engage the children in observing and doing. In darker, larger print, directions for activities are provided for the children. Activities include terrariums, botany experiments, window boxes, gardening, sunflower cultivation, and plant crafts.

Kavaler, Lucy. *Green Magic: Algae Rediscovered.* Crowell, 1983. 120 pp. (I). RMA 6.2.

This book describes the earliest plant life and provides a timetable with references to dinosaurs. Plants in space are also discussed.

Keats, Ezra Jack. *Clementina's Cactus.* Viking, 1982. (P). 32 pp. RMA 6.3.

In this wordless book, Clementina discovers a cactus in the desert. After a thunderstorm brings rain to the desert, the cactus bursts into bloom.

Keller, Beverly. *The Beetle Bush.* Coward, McCann & Geoghegan, 1976. 64 pp. (P). RMA 8.3.

Arabelle experiences failure after failure. She's a very discouraged little girl until her father suggests that she grow a garden. It does quite well until the weeds, moles, snails, and beetles begin to take over. When the landlord comes to visit, Arabelle makes a decision to treat the weeds and critters as useful and positive. The landlord is so impressed by her attitude as well as her critter collection that he brings his son along on his next visit. All have a great time enjoying Arabelle's garden, and Arabelle experiences a sense of accomplishment when they discover a watermelon that has grown among the weeds. This easy-to-read book will bring encouragement to all.

Kellogg, Cynthia. *Corn: What It Is, What It Does.* Greenwillow, 1989. 47 pp. (P). RMA 4.5.

The title says it all. The author provides young readers with the facts about the history, lore, propagation, and uses of corn.

Kelsey, Elin. *Nature's Children: Bees.* Grolier, 1985, 47 pp. (P-I). RMA 10.3.

Have you ever wondered what was going on inside a honeybee's well-defended hive? In Kelsey's text enhanced by color photos, a two-page labeled picture reveals all. She describes the life cycle and habits of the honeybee.

Kerby, Mona. *Friendly Bees, Ferocious Bees.* Watts, 1987. 96 pp. (I). RMA 10.3.

In addition to basic information about bees, pictures and text present various styles of hives and directions for building a bee-catching box. Of particular interest is the identification and description of the seven bee dances by which the messenger bee tells the hive where a food source may be found. Finally, titles for further reading, a glossary, cooking tips, and recipes for honey are included.

Kimmel, Eric. *Anansi and the Talking Melon.* Holiday House, 1994. 32 pp. Illustrated by Janet Stevens. (P-I). RMA 9.5.

Anansi, the legendary spider, decided one day to have fun with Elephant. Inasmuch as he was stuck inside one of Elephant's melons, he thought it would be fun to play a trick on Elephant. When Elephant picked the melon, Anansi screamed, "Ouch!" The astonished Elephant decided that a talking melon must be seen by the king, so an adventure was launched. This amusing tale from an African garden is perfect for storytelling.

King, Elizabeth. *Backyard Sunflower.* Dutton, 1993. 32 pp. (P). RMA 3.3.

Samantha plants and nurtures a sunflower patch. Her joy and care are documented by King's photographs. This book cheers you up just by looking at it.

King, Elizabeth. *The Pumpkin Patch.* Dutton, 1990. 40 pp. (P). RMA 4.2.

In a straightforward documentary fashion this photographic picture book tells the story of a commercial pumpkin patch operation in southern California. The photographs portray the progression from the preparation of the field to the planting of treated seeds, the weeding, the harvesting, and the selling.

Kirkus, Virginia. *The First Book of Gardening.* Watts, 1956. 78 pp. (P). RMA 8.4.

An old but valuable book, this work can probably still be found in school and public libraries. It contains information that cannot be found in newer books for young gardeners; in particular, the section on tools is more substantial than others written for the primary-age set. The text takes the young gardener through the first year of starting a garden. Invaluable and handy for all gardeners are the illustrations showing the first leaves of plants so gardeners don't weed out the flowers and cultivate the weeds when a garden has newly sprouted.

Kohl, Mary Ann, and Cindy Gainer. *Good Earth Art.* Bright Ring, 1991. 224 pp. (I). RMA 1.2, 8.5.

A collection of numerous kid-tested ideas that use natural items as the media. Some of these ideas include creating nature scenes from items gathered during a nature walk; making vegie garlands, gourd guitars, and berry dyes; and weaving with cattails and branches. A good buy for adults who need environmental art activities to engage children's hands and minds.

Kramer, Jack. *Plant Sculptures.* Morrow, 1978. 63 pp. (I). RMA 8.2.

Kramer states on the first page that this activity may take two to six months to complete and requires patience. That stated, he describes how to create animal shapes from 14- to 16-inch gauge wire; these shapes become the armature upon which plants, such as *Ficus pumila, Hypocyrta strigilosa,* and *Columnea arguta,* grow. An adult who wishes to do these projects with larger groups of children should enlist several other adult helpers. The thought of 30 undersupervised 11-year-olds whipping around 15-gauge wire gives one pause. Kramer wrote this book for individual youths seeking a new hobby.

Krasilovsky, Phyllis. *The First Tulips in Holland.* Doubleday, 1982. 32 pp. (P-I). RMA 3.2.

A merchant, seeking to make money, brings tulips from Persia to Holland in this fictional account.

Krauss, Ruth. *The Carrot Seed.* HarperCollins, 1945. (P). RMA 2.3.

Still a favorite among the preschool and kindergarten set, this is the story of a young boy who plants a carrot seed and waits patiently for the sprouts.

Krementz, Jill. *A Very Young Gardener.* Dial, 1991. 34 pp. (P). RMA 7.3.

Krementz's photojournalist's eye reveals the young gardener's thoughtful and enthusiastic planning, planting, and tending of her garden. The parent's support and pride in her accomplishments come shining through the photographs.

Kuhn, Dwight. *More Than Just a Vegetable Garden.* Silver Press, 1990. 40 pp. (P-I). RMA 10.4.

This photographic look at the changing world of the vegetable garden and the creatures that inhabit it includes simple instructions for starting a garden.

L

Laird, Elizabeth. *Rosy's Garden: A Child's Keepsake of Flowers*. Philomel Books, 1990. (P-I). 46 pp. Illustrated by Satomi Ichikawa. RMA 3.1. 5.3.

Rosy visited her grandmother and learned about flowers and gardening. This treasure includes the lore, poetry, crafts, and games associated with plants, including tulips, roses and herbs. The text is by Elizabeth Laird; the illustrations are by Satomi Ichikawa, who has top billing. When looking it up in your library or bookstore, try both names.

Lauber, Patricia. *Seeds: Pop, Stick, Glide*. Crown, 1981. 57 pp. (P-I). Photographs by Jerome Wexler. RMA 2.3.

If seeds were human, they'd need passports. They love to travel. Lauber tells us how they do it. Jerome Wexler's close-up photographs show the reader seeds with burrs, jelly-covered seeds, seeds that are animal food, seeds that travel on the wind, salt shaker seeds, seeds with wings, and seeds that float on water. Wexler's photographs capture the process so readers can easily see what is going on with seed travelers.

Lavies, Bianca. *Backyard Hunter: The Praying Mantis*. Dutton, 1990. 32 pp. (I). RMA 9.2.

Photographs document a thorough discussion of the behavior, life cycle, and development of the insect-eating praying mantis, a beneficial insect for the gardener.

Lavies, Bianca. *Compost Critters*. Dutton, 1993. 30 pp. (I). RMA 7.2.

Magnified close-up photographs reveal the inhabitants of a compost pile—sow bugs, earthworms, nematodes, mites, and millipedes. Lavies helps children appreciate the value of nature's recyclers.

Lee, Jeanne M. *Toad Is the Uncle of Heaven: A Vietnamese Folk Tale*. Henry Holt, 1985. 32 pp. (I). RMA 9.4.

This simple story tells how the toad became the Vietnamese symbol of rain.

Leedy, Loreen. *The Potato Party and Other Troll Tales*. Holiday House, 1989. 32 pp. (P). RMA 4.4.

This Scandinavian tale shows what happens when you have nothing to eat but potatoes, potatoes, potatoes every night.

Lember, Barbara Hirsch. *A Book of Fruit*. Ticknor & Fields, 1994. 32 pp. (P). RMA 5.5.

A true picture book of few words, it presents pairs of photos: One photo shows the fruit, the accompanying one shows a full shot of the orchard, bog, or grove in which the fruit grew.

Lenski, Lois. *Strawberry Girl*. Dell, 1945. 194 pp. (I). RMA 5.4.

In another of Lenski's regional stories, the author shows the sweet and violent sides of Florida's rural working poor during the early 1900s. Birdie Boyer and her family grow strawberries to be shipped to northern markets. Just as an aside, this was one of Oprah Winfrey's favorite books when she was in fourth grade.

Lerner, Carol. *Dumb Cane and Daffodils: Poisonous Plants in the House and Garden*. Morrow, 1990. 32 pp. (I). RMA 1.1.

Now here is a book that children should read before they begin to garden and work with plants. This informative book describes more than 30 indoor and garden plants hazardous to humans and pets.

Lerner, Carol. *Flowers of a Woodland Spring*. Morrow, 1979. 28 pp. (I). RMA 3.5.

Exquisite drawings and watercolors by Lerner show the beauty of ephemerals. Lerner tells and shows the underground life of woodland flowers in addition to identifying these common flowers that brighten the shade.

Lerner, Carol. *Pitcher Plants: The Elegant Insect Traps*. Morrow, 1983. 64 pp. (I). RMA 6.4.

Lerner describes and illustrates eight species that grow in North America. Pitcher plants belong to the family of carnivorous (flesh-eating) plants. Carnivorous plants are also referred to as insectivorous (insect-eating) plants. They grow in wetlands, such as bogs, marshes, swamps, and coastal areas in North and South America, Asia, and Australia.

Lerner, Carol. *Plant Families*. Morrow, 1989. 32 pp. (I). **2.5.**

Lerner's detailed illustrations provide aesthetic botany lessons as she introduces 12 of the largest plant families to young readers. Lerner sorts out the *Compositae* from the *Umbelliferai*; the *Rosaceae* from the *Labiatae*. Each plant has particular characteristics that place it in one category but not another, as botanists classify the plants. Lerner tells her readers how this is done. Before this book is introduced to readers, it is recommended that they have read a more basic botany book, such as *What's Inside? Plants* by Angela Royston, so that they know how to identify plant parts.

Le Tord, Bijou. *Rabbit Seeds*. Four Winds, 1984. 32 pp. (P). RMA 7.5.

What does a gardener do? We are told in simple language and black and white pen-and-ink drawings in this story about a rabbit gardener.

Lindberg, Reeve. *Johnny Appleseed.* Little, Brown, 1990. 32 pp. (I). RMA 1.3.

A biographical poem and folk art convey the story of John Chapman (1774-1845), a naturalist and missionary who distributed apple seeds from his nursery to settlers of the American frontier.

Lionni, Leo. *Six Crows: A Fable.* Knopf, 1988. 32 pp. (P). RMA 8.1.

This picture book tells the story of the owl who resolves the problem between the farmer and the crows who eat the farmer's wheat.

Littlewood, Valerie. *Scarecrow!* Dutton, 1992. 29 pp. (P-I). **8.1.**

Gardeners are always seeking ways to control pests such as birds. Littlewood documents the devices and strategies employed by various cultures—British clappers, Japanese kakashi—to chase away pests. The history, lore, and crafts of scarecrows are described in this illustrated book. Littlewood includes easy-to-follow directions for scarecrow construction.

Lobel, Anita. *Alison's Zinnia.* Greenwillow, 1990. 32 pp. (P). **3.4.**

Richly colored floral art by Anita Lobel captures the reader's eye as linked sentences take us through the book. A gift to both teachers and gardeners, the storyline sets up an opportunity for sentence pattern practice—name-verb-flower—upon which alternative activities may be built. Worth noting is the author-illustrator's explanation about how the book came to be.

Lobel, Arnold. *Frog and Toad Together.* Harper & Row, 1971. 63 pp. (P). **9.4.**

Use this beloved classic as a springboard to the study of frogs and toads. Chapters are self-contained stories that can be read independent of the others. The second chapter, "The Garden," features Toad as the impatient gardener waiting for his seeds to grow.

Lobel, Arnold. *The Rose in My Garden.* Morrow, 1993. 40 pp. (P-I). Illustrated by Anita Lobel. **3.1.**

Using the cumulative tale style of traditional folk literature, the story follows a bee that falls asleep on a rose as the tale teller adds flower after flower. Eventually, a cat comes along to bring the tale to a close with a surprise ending. Anita Lobel's lush floral illustrations make this droll tale a treasure. Youth leaders seeking ways to increase children's ability to play with language will appreciate the text.

Lottridge, Celia Barker. *One Watermelon Seed.* Oxford, 1986. 24 pp. (P). Illustrated by Karen Patkau. RMA 11.2.

From Canada comes this delightful counting book based on a gardening theme. It takes the reader from 1 to 10 and then by 10s to 100.

Lovejoy, Sharon. *Hollyhock Days.* Interweave Press, 1994. 95 pp. (I). RMA 3.3, 8.2, 9.5, 10.1.

The sequel to *Sunflower Houses,* this is an equally enchanting book to be enjoyed by older children, who will want to try creating hollyhock houses and caterpillar tents.

Lovejoy, Sharon. *Sunflower Houses: Garden Discoveries for Children of All Ages.* Interweave Press, 1991. 44 pp. (I). RMA 3.3, 8.2, 11.2.

Are you seeking ideas for thematic gardens? Are you looking for toys in the garden? Are you seeking soul-satisfying essays about gardening? These and more are to be found in this charming book written in a spirit of love and remembrance for a grandmother's garden. Lovejoy describes how to make sunflower houses and other garden delights. References to growing mini-vegetables are scattered throughout.

M

Mallett, David. *Inch by Inch: The Garden Song.* Harper-Collins, 1995. 26 pp. (P). Illustrated by Ora Eitan. RMA 7.2, &.3.

The song sung by gardeners everywhere is illustrated here in warm colors. The musical score is provided at the end of the text.

Manton, Jo, and Robert Gittings. "The Peach Blossom Forest." In *The Flying Horses: Tales from China.* Holt, Rinehart & Winston, 1977. 172 pp. (I). RMA 5.2.

Ying, a poor fisherman, discovers a land of great beauty and peace in which a peach blossom forest grows. When he breaks his promise not to tell anyone where the peach blossom forest is located, it disappears. This is an ancient tale from the fourth century.

Markmann, Erika. *Grow It! An Indoor/Outdoor Gardening Guide for Kids.* Random House, 1991. 47 pp. (P-I). Illustrated by Gisela Konemund. **8.2;** RMA 1.4, 2.4, 11.1, 11.4.

For the city gardener, Markmann's book gives good information about growing, caring for, and propagating indoor plants. She even provides good advice to children about how to care for their plants when they go on vacation. She encourages city children to garden outdoors on balconies, porches, and terraces. She also shows children how to build a silver lace vine tipi.

Marsh, Janet. *A Child's Book of Flowers.* Hutchinson, 1993. 59 pp. (I). RMA 3.1.

Charming illustrations and text present botany, history, folklore, poetry, games, and activities related to 25 favorite flowers.

Mayes, Susan. *What Makes a Flower Grow?* Usborne House, 1989. 24 pp. (P). RMA 2.1.

The author explains botany basics in language young children can comprehend. Plant parts, pollination, seed development, seed travel, and germination are covered. This is an excellent book for beginning readers.

McCloskey, Robert. *Blueberries for Sal.* Viking, 1948. 54 pp. (P). **5.5.**

Little Sal and her mother and Little Bear and his mother go off for a day of blueberry gathering and eating. They become separated and mixed up but eventually get back together with their own mothers, and the story ends happily.

McDonald, Megan. *The Great Pumpkin Switch.* Orchard, 1992. 32 pp. (P-I). **4.2.**

Grandpa tells a story from his childhood about the time he and his friend Otto accidentally cut his sister Rosie's special Big Max pumpkin from the vine. They were in big trouble. Fortunately, they recovered by purchasing an equally handsome big pumpkin from Mr. Angelo.

McDonald, Megan. *The Potato Man.* Orchard, 1991. 32 pp. (P-I). RMA 4.4.

In this story from the early 1900s, Grandpa recalls the time when he and his friend Otto encountered The Potato Man, a vegetable peddler. One-eyed with a disfigured face, The Potato Man frightened the children by his appearance. The children retaliated by teasing him and stealing from his wagon. Bad luck followed until The Potato Man returned their childish meanness with a kindness.

McLaughlin, Molly. *Earthworms, Dirt, and Rotten Leaves.* Atheneum, 1986. 86 pp. (I). RMA 9.1.

This guide to earthworms contains a diagram and do-it-yourself experiments. It also includes a good chapter about the food chain.

McMillan, Bruce. *Counting Wildflowers.* Lothrop, Lee & Shepard, 1986. 28 pp. (P). RMA 3.5.

This is a counting book from 1 to 20 with beautiful, full-color wildflower photographs. Other counting books in this bibliography include *One Watermelon Seed.*

McNulty, Faith. *The Lady and the Spider.* HarperCollins, 1986. 44 pp. (P). Illustrated by Bob Marstall. RMA 9.5.

After reading this story, children will have an enhanced appreciation for all life, no matter how tiny and fragile. A spider comes to live on a lettuce plant, happily surviving on the insects there. One day the gardener picks the lettuce for her lunch. Admiring the spider, she frees it.

Meltzer, Milton. *The Amazing Potato.* HarperCollins, 1992. 116 pp. (I). **4.4.**

Award-winning history writer Milton Meltzer focuses his talent on the potato, a lowly vegetable to which millions in the world owe their existence. Is that a grandiose claim? After reading this book that tells of the potato's origins, history, cultivation requirements, and economic significance, children are likely to be impressed with this vegetable, which has a worldwide market value of 100 billion dollars. Teachers, especially of intermediate grade social studies, will appreciate the ease with which they can construct an integrated curriculum around this theme.

Micucci, Charles. *The Life and Times of the Apple.* Orchard Books, 1992. 32 pp. (P-I). RMA 5.1.

This book includes apple history, lore, life cycles, uses, and modern growing practices.

Milord, Susan. *The Kids' Nature Book: 365 Indoor/Outdoor Activities and Experiences.* Williamson, 1989. 158 pp. (I). RMA 1.4, 8.5.

An activity for every day of the year. Susan Milord has compiled nature-study, gardening, and craft activities that will keep the antsy 8- to 12-year-old happy and occupied.

Mintz, Lorelie M. *How to Grow Fruits and Berries.* Messner, 1980. 96 pp. (I). RMA 5.5.

Detailed explanations of fruit tree and berry bush planting and cultivation are given. Pruning techniques are given good coverage. Apple, grapefruit, cherry, blueberry, figs, and avocado cultivation are among the many varieties covered by this practical book.

Mintz, Lorelie M. *Vegetables in Patches and Pots.* Farrar, Straus & Giroux, 1976. 116 pp. (I). RMA 7.5.

A comprehensive guide to organic vegetable gardening, the emphasis in this book is on natural pest control, good soil management, and timing. A guide to individual vegetable varieties and their care follows the how-to-garden section. Of particular value to city gardeners is her chapter about growing vegetables in odd containers. The seventies was a high point for books about organic gardening for children, so persevere in your search for this one on public library shelves.

Mitchell, Andrew. *The Young Naturalist.* Usborne House, 1989. 32 pp. (P). RMA 1.2.

Information and activities for the young naturalist include experiments with plants, looking at flowers and trees, inviting animals to visit you, making and using collections, and nature through the camera's eye.

Moore, Elaine. *Grandma's Garden.* Lothrop, Lee & Shepard, 1994. 32 pp. (P-I). Illustrations by Dan Andreasen. RMA 8.3.

When Kim visits her grandmother, they share the anticipation and problems of planting the garden. Problems arise and they find solutions, from making scarecrows and replanting a washed-out garden to spraying the plum trees with water to prevent frost damage. A story of warmth and caring.

Motomara, Mitchell. *Momotaro*. Raintree, 1989. 32 pp. (P). Illustrated by Kyuzo Tsugami. **5.2.**
A childless couple is delighted to find a baby boy in a giant peach. They name the child Momotaro. They live happily until ogres invade their village and steal all their belongings. Momotaro pursues the ogres to their homeland. With the aid of a dog, a monkey, and a pheasant, he overcomes the ogres and retrieves the family's possessions.

Mound, Laurence. *Insect*. Knopf, 1990. 64 pp. (I). RMA 9.2.
Describes insect anatomy, particular species, and how insects survive and relate to other living things.

Muller, Gerda. *The Garden in the City*. Dutton, 1992. 40 pp. (P-I). **11.4.**
Originally published in Germany, this book shows readers how Caroline and Ben planted and cared for their backyard gardens in the city. They get help from Luke, a physically disabled child who gardens on a balcony above their backyard. The story unfolds as the seasons pass. Craft directions and recipes are woven into the seams of the narrative.

N

Namioka, Lensey. *Valley of the Broken Cherry Trees*. Delacorte, 1980. 218 pp. (I). RMA 5.3.
Method, motive, and opportunity, the three elements of whodunits, are all here; only this time the victims in this horticultural mystery set in medieval Japan are cherry trees. Zenta, along with his sidekick Matsuko, seeks to find out who damaged the much-admired cherry trees. Intrigue abounds in this historical fiction adventure story.

Norsgaard, E. Jaediker. *Nature's Great Balancing Act: In Our Own Backyard*. Cobblehill, 1990. 64 pp. (I). RMA 10.5.
The interrelationships of plants, animals, insects, and birds are explored in a semi-wild New England backyard.

O

O'Callahan, Jay. *Tulips*. Picture Book Studio, 1992. 26 pp. (P). Illustrated by Debrah Santini. RMA 3.2.
Storyteller O'Callahan treats gardening children to this story about a young man who loves to play tricks on people. His Grand Ma Mere grows the most beautiful tulips in all of Paris. He decides to play a gardener's trick on his Grand Ma Mere but finds that the tables are turned on him. A great story to use for storytelling.

Ocone, Lynn, with Eve Pranis. *National Gardening Association Guide to Kids' Gardening*. Wiley, 1990. 148 pp. (I). **8.3;** RMA 8.4, 8.5, 11.5.
One of the most authoritative books about children's gardening on today's market. It not only covers basic gardening completely but also makes connections to other curricular areas, including science. This book is considered to be a bible for starting up school and community garden programs.

Overbeck, Cynthia. *Cactus*. Lerner, 1982. 48 pp. (P-I). RMA 6.3.
This book features Sonoran cacti with recipes and suggestions for raising the plant.

Overbeck, Cynthia. *Carnivorous Plants*. Lerner, 1982. 48 pp. (I). RMA 6.4.
Color photos and descriptive text introduce a wide range of carnivorous plants, including the waterwheel, pitcher plant, and Venus's fly trap, and explain how they attract and trap small insects.

Overbeck, Cynthia. *How Seeds Travel*. Lerner, 1982. 48 pp. (P-I). RMA 2.3.
Photographs and text introduce the structure of the seed and flower. Overbeck shows how seeds are carried by the air, by animals, and by water.

Overbeck, Cynthia. *Sunflower*. Lerner, 1981. 48 pp. (I). RMA 3.3.
Color photos and labeled diagrams augment the readable text to present a detailed description of the sunflower's life cycle. Phototropism, the tendency to bend toward light, is described as this relates to the sunflower. Because the sunflower needs as much energy as possible from the sun, the plants lean toward it and follow its light throughout the day. The direction the plant is leaning may be used to tell the time of day.

P

Pallotta, Jerry. *The Flower Alphabet Book*. Charlesbridge, 1988. 32 pp. (P). Illustrated by Leslie Evans. RMA 3.4.
This is one of several science-related alphabet books by this author. Leslie Evans's gorgeous and brilliant illustrations and her detailed, fascinating notes about the lore of the flowers illustrated will appeal to young readers as well as adults.

Parker, Alice. *Terrariums.* Watts, 1977. 46 pp. (P-I). **1.5.**

The copyright may be old, but the information is excellent. Still to be found on library shelves, Parker's terrarium-construction directions are easy to follow. She describes step by step the preparation of three types of terrariums: woodland, tropical, and desert. She also tells about the necessary equipment, materials, and plants appropriate for each. The book includes hints for the care of each type.

Parker, Nancy Winslow, and Joan Richard Wright. *Frogs, Toads, Lizards, and Salamanders.* Greenwillow, 1990. 48 pp. (P-I). RMA 9.3, 9.4.

Sixteen amphibians and reptiles found in the United States are featured. Using a two-page-spread format, a cartoon and couplet appear on the left and a labeled drawing and basic information on the right. Scientific drawings are carefully labeled with simple symbols. Final pages include range maps, a glossary, diagrams, a scientific classification chart, and a bibliography.

Parnall, Peter. *The Daywatchers.* Macmillan, 1985. 127 pp. (I). RMA 10.2.

This personalized introduction to birds of prey is based on the author's years of birdwatching and is illustrated with birds in their natural habitats.

Parsons, Alexandra. *Amazing Spiders.* Knopf, 1990. 29 pp. (P-I). Photographs by Jerry Young. RMA 9.5.

This factual presentation of spider life and habits is enhanced by Young's photographs.

Patent, Dorothy Hinshaw. *An Apple a Day: From Orchard to You.* Cobblehill, 1990. 64 pp. (I). Photographs by William Munoz. **5.1.**

A comprehensive account of the six varieties of apples that comprise over 80 percent of the United States crop, the text also describes cultivation procedures. It covers propagation, tree shaping, blossoms, the role of bees, combatting pests, harvesting, storing, sorting, packing, and selling. The orchards of Yakima, Washington, are featured. With this in mind, a good companion book would be *Apple Picking Time* by Michele Benoit Slawson, a Yakima Valley native.

Paul, Aileen. *Kids Outdoor Gardening.* Doubleday, 1978. 77 pp. (I). RMA 8.2, 11.2.

Paul provides the necessary information for the youthful gardener to get started with this popular home-based hobby that is likely to last a lifetime. She talks about tools, compost, succession planting, and planting by the moon. Included are the directions for a play tent of chicken wire, posts, and gourd vines.

Pellowski, Anne. *The Story Vine.* Collier Books, 1984. 116 pp. (I). RMA 1.3.

Action stories from around the world include string, picture drawing, sand, and fingerplay stories, as well as stories using dolls, riddles, and musical instruments.

Perenyi, Constance. *Growing Wild.* Beyond Words, 1991. 39 pp. (I). **10.5;** RMA 11.3.

Using paper-cutout illustrations, Perenyi tells how a lawn evolved from a clipped and perfect suburban lawn to a wild and weedy wildlife refuge. After the story is told, projects follow with lists of resources and organizations that support the notion of turning yards into refuges for birds and insects.

Petie, Haris. *The Seed the Squirrel Dropped.* Prentice-Hall, 1976. 32 pp. (P). RMA 5.3.

In cumulative tale fashion, a seed-to-cherry-tree-to-cherry-tart story is told. The recipe for the tart is included. This is a charming book that should not be overlooked.

Pike, Norman. *The Peach Tree.* Stemmer, 1983. 32 pp. (P). RMA. 5.2.

When the aphids begin to weaken the Pomeroys' peach tree, ladybugs are brought in to eat the aphids. The peach tree is saved. This book mixes science with fantasy, so readers need to take care to know which is which. The interdependence among insects, plants, and humans is shown.

Pohl, Kathleen. *Tulips.* Steck-Vaughn, 1986. 32 pp. (P-I). RMA 3.2.

The life cycle of tulips is presented and developed through photographs and readable text.

Politi, Leo. *Three Stalks of Corn.* Scribner's, 1993. 32 pp. (P-I). **4.5.**

In Pico Rivera, California, Angelica lives with her *abuelita,* Mrs. Corrales. Grandmother likes to garden; she plants all the ingredients, including corn, needed for the Mexican food that she makes so well. Mrs. Corrales passes on the rich Hispanic culture and customs to her granddaughter. She tells her the ancient legends of Mexico, especially as these relate to corn. She teaches Angelica how to make hot chocolate, tortillas, tacos, and enchiladas. The school principal invites Angelica's *abuelita* to show the other children how to make tortillas and tacos. Recipes for these are included.

Pope, Joyce. *Plant Partnerships.* Facts on File, 1990. 62 pp. (I). RMA 2.2, 6.4.

Using a two-page-spread format, this book features flesh-eating plants, such as bladder-wort, butterworts, pitcher plants, sundew, and Venus's fly traps. Brief explanations of how and why the plants obtain nutrients from insects are provided.

Porter, Wes. *The Garden Book.* Workman, 1989. 64 pp. (P-I). **7.5;** RMA 1.5.

The book's designer knew that children would be dragging his little book (4" x 6") into the garden. It has a laminated cover to protect it. Full of practical suggestions, it tells how to create productive soil, how pollination works, how to plan a garden, how to transplant, and how to care for plants in the garden. Written for both the outdoor and indoor gardener, it contains a section on house plants and terrariums.

Priceman, Marjorie. *How to Make an Apple Pie and See the World.* Knopf, 1994. 32 pp. (P). RMA 5.1.

Children gain a lesson in geography and world agriculture as they find out how to make an apple pie in this whimsical picture book.

Pringle, Laurence. *Killer Bees.* Morrow, 1990. 56 pp. (I). RMA 10.3.

Killer Bees surveys the effect of the African honeybee on South and Central America and examines its impact on the United States. This revision of *Here Come the Killer Bees* delineates the challenges and changes that this invasion presents and the threat it poses to the honey and agricultural industries.

Pulver, Robin. *Nobody's Mother Is in Second Grade.* Dial, 1992. 32 pp. (P). Illustrated by G. Brian Karas. RMA 1.1.

Cassandra's mother wants to visit second grade but Cassandra doesn't want her mother there. Mom disguises herself as a house plant for her visit. Plays on words and comparisons between plants and people abound in this humorous book that invites language lessons.

Q

Quattlebaum, Mary. *Jackson Jones and the Puddle of Thorns.* Delacorte, 1994. 113 pp. (I). RMA 11.5.

More than anything else, Jackson Jones wants a new basketball. His birthday is coming up and he can barely wait. His mother, who misses the country life of her childhood, wants her son to have the happiness she knew as a child when she had a garden. She gives Jackson Plot 5-1 at the Rooter's Community Garden. Not exactly a basketball! Jackson not only handles it well, he figures out a way to turn his plot into a business success, but not before he solves some problems he encounters with friends and one enemy, Blood Green. Multicultural urban lifestyles are realistically and humorously portrayed.

R

Raferty, Kevin, and Kim G. Raferty. *Kids Gardening: A Kid's Guide to Messing Around in the Dirt.* Klutz Press, 1989. 87 pp. (P-I). **7.3;** RMA 1.4, 7.4.

With a lighthearted approach, this all-year activity guide introduces the basics of indoor/outdoor gardening. The tagboard pages and plastic ring binder permit the young gardener to take this book into the garden. In addition to basic gardening—soil preparation, planting seeds, weeding, and watering—the book also contains information about scarecrows, worm farms, and kitchen gardening. Plants are partnered with projects; garlic cultivation with plaiting garlic braids, for example.

Rahn, Joan Elma. *Nature in the City: Plants.* Raintree, 1971. 47 pp. (P-I). RMA 11.3.

Eighteen commonly found plants of city sidewalks and empty lots are named and described. Younger readers can gain information from the photographs.

Rapp, Joel. *Let's Get Growing.* Prince Paperbacks, 1993. 96 pp. (I). **2.4;** RMA 6.2, 7.4.

Rapp has written up 25 activities for children to try with both indoor and outdoor plants. Included are rose culture, cactus grafting, terrarium making, and air layering, as well as basic gardening procedures.

Rhoades, Diane. *Garden Crafts for Kids: 50 Great Reasons to Get Your Hands Dirty.* Sterling/Lark, 1995. 144 pp. (I). **9.3;** RMA 7.1, 7.3, 7.4.

The perfect book! Just right for children and for all of us who garden with children. Beautifully designed, it invites readers to browse through the pages, harvesting idea after idea. Rhoades has written one of the best chapters about designing gardens. Children will discover how to design a garden, the various shapes that gardens may have, and the many considerations that gardeners need to keep in mind as they plan their gardens.

The first six chapters provide detailed directions for establishing, designing, planting, and caring for a garden. Chapter 7 describes dozens of kid-tested, appealing craft ideas—some practical, some decorative, and all doable. Included are toilet paper seed tape, rustic trellises, shoe scrapers, and worm condos. Rhoades includes guidelines for setting up and maintaining a produce stand. Combined with the information from Swenson's *Big Fun to Grow* book, this book will help children become entrepreneurs as well as gardeners. Recipes are also featured. Apple leather is sure to appeal.

Photographs of children making the projects and working in their gardens clarify the text and inspire replication by children. Bright, attractive, and informative, this book is definitely in the top 10 of current children's gardening books.

Ricciuti, Edward. *Plants in Danger.* Harper & Row, 1979. 86 pp. (I). RMA 6.4.

This book begins with the story of a cactus seed that fell to the ground near the Spanish garrison town of Tucson, Arizona. The growth of the seed into a 200-year-old, 50-foot saguaro cactus parallels the growth of Tucson to a modern city. In this storylike manner, using an historical perspective, the author examines both natural changes and destructive threats occurring to plant life in environments around the world and discusses the value of plant diversity.

Richardson, Joy. *Flowers.* Watts, 1993. 29 pp. (P). RMA 3.1.

In very simple text and color photographs, Richardson provides basic information about flowers for the primer set.

Robbins, Ken. *A Flower Grows.* Dial, 1988. 32 pp. (P-I). **3.2.**

This picture book shows the growth of an amaryllis. A series of paintings shows the bud about to bloom, the unfolding, and then the fading of the flower. Replenishment of the bulb's food supply by the remaining green leaves is explained. Instructions with illustrations for planting and raising the bulb are given. After sharing the story, grow your own amaryllis. This rapidly growing flower provides a dramatic introduction to bulbs.

Robson, Denny, and Vanessa Bailey. *Rainy Days Grow It for Fun.* Gloucester Press, 1991. 32 pp. (P-I). RMA 1.1.

Robson and Bailey convey information about gardening indoors. Their house plant and indoor gardening projects include mushroom cultivation, air plants, dish gardens, and terrarium and aquarium gardening.

Rockwell, Harlow. *The Compost Heap.* Doubleday, 1974. 24 pp. (P). **7.2.**

In this book for very young readers, composting is made simple enough for the preschool set to understand and do. Simple cartoonlike drawings in soft colors illustrate the storyline about a young boy and his father working together through the seasons making and maintaining a compost pile.

Roth, Susan L. *The Story of Light.* Morrow, 1990. 32 pp. (P-I). RMA 9.5.

A Cherokee Indian myth of how Spider captured a piece of the sun and brought it to the animal people.

Royston, Angela. *What's Inside? Plants.* Dorling Kindersley, 1992. 17 pp. (P). RMA 2.1.

This brightly colored, easy book is part of the What's Inside? series. Large, simple drawings of the inside of various plant life-forms reveal how plants make and transport food, as well as take up water. The function of plant parts is explained. Excellent coverage of botany for young children.

Ryder, Joanne. *Dancers in the Garden.* Sierra Club, 1992. 32 pp. (P-I). Illustrated by Judith Lopaz. RMA 10.2.

Inspired by Golden Gate Park, the exquisite oriental-style paintings by Judith Lopaz and Ryder's poetic text convey the lovely story of two hummingbirds' courtship dance.

Ryder, Joanne. *The Spiders Dance.* Harper, 1981. 40 pp. (P-I). Illustrated by Robert Blake. **9.5.**

Ryder's poetry tells the story of a spider's life. Illustrations of blue, green, and yellow portray tiny spiders emerging from their silken nest. Soon they weave webs, trap food, grow, mate, and lay their own eggs. This charming book is sure to engage the interest of both girls and boys across age levels. After reading this book, children may be interested in learning that the tarantella dance was named after the tarantula. It would make a good nonfiction companion to *Charlotte's Web*.

Ryder, Joanne. *Where Butterflies Grow.* Dutton, 1989. 32 pp. (P-I). Illustrated by Lynne Cherry. RMA 10.1.

Lynne Cherry's lush wildflower meadow pictures provide the background for Joanne Ryder's poem, which invites children to imagine that they are butterflies. Ryder takes readers from the caterpillar emerging from a tiny egg, to spinning a cocoon, to breaking out of the cocoon as a lovely black swallowtail butterfly. It is the perfect book for adult leaders and classroom teachers who are involving their children in a butterfly-raising project. The last page of the book describes how to raise and care for a caterpillar and how to grow a butterfly garden. The book combines science, poetry, and art as only Ryder and Cherry can.

S

Sakade, Florence. "Peach Boy." In *Japanese Children's Favorite Stories*. Charles E. Tuttle, 1958. 120 pp. (I). RMA 5.2.

This is a retelling of the Momotaro story.

Samson, Suzanne. *Fairy Dusters and Blazing Stars*. Roberts Rinehart, 1994. 32 pp. (P-I). Illustrated by Preston Neel. RMA 3.5.

A fanciful treatment of exploring wildflowers with children, this book pairs descriptive wildflower names, such as pussy paws, with an illustration playing on the words. The downside is that for many children the actual wildflower may be inaccessible—some grow in the Baja desert, in high-elevation forests in northern California, or along western mountain stream banks. For those who enjoy playing with words, however, the book is fun.

San Souci, Robert. *Feathertop*. Doubleday, 1992. 32 pp. (P-I). Illustrated by Daniel San Souci. RMA 8.1.
  This retelling of Nathaniel Hawthorne's old tale of a witch's revenge is beautifully illustrated by Daniel San Souci.

Savage, Candace, and Gary Clement. *Get Growing*. Firefly, 1991. 56 pp. (I). RMA 7.1.
  Written from an ecological perspective, *Get Growing* encourages care of the soil and water. Soil contamination and water pollution causes and solutions are addressed.

Schaefer, Carole Lexa. *In the Children's Garden*. Henry Holt, 1994. 32 pp. (P). Illustrated by Lynn Pauley. RMA 11.4.
  This picture book captures the spirit and joy of children gardening in the city. The five senses are evoked. The narration ends with an invitation to children to plant another children's garden. Pauley's bright, rich palette creates a charming, attractive book.

Schertle, Alice. *Witch Hazel*. HarperCollins, 1991. 32 pp. (P). Illustrated by Margot Tomes. RMA 8.1.
  Johnny plants pumpkin seeds and then needs a scarecrow. His brothers Bill and Bart cut a witch hazel branch that Johnny dresses in a gingham dress and makes his scarecrow. Hazel guards the pumpkin until it becomes orange and round. Then one night she tosses it into the sky and dances by the light of the harvest moon.

Schnieper, Claudia. *Chameleons*. Carolrhoda, 1989. 47 pp. (P-I). RMA 9.3.
  Color photos augment the readable text, which discusses the characteristics, different species, reproduction, diet, and habitats of chameleons.

Schwartz, Alvin. *Busy Buzzing Bumble Bees and Other Tongue Twisters*. Harper & Row, 1982. 63 pp. RMA 14.3.
  This collection of 46 tongue twisters is sure to be a source of fun-filled word play.

Schwartz, David M. *The Hidden Life of the Meadow*. Crown, 1988. 40 pp. (P-I). RMA 10.4.
  Schwartz depicts the plant life of a wild meadow as well as the animals there.

Sedenko, Jerry. *The Butterfly Garden*. Villard, 1991. 144 pp. (I). **10.1.**
  The author shares his love of butterflies and gardens in this informative resource book augmented by full-color photos. The preface includes history, folklore, and even poetry. Sedenko describes the life cycle of butterflies and provides guides to butterflies, flowers, and plants with suggestions and designs for the butterfly garden. Finally, he includes appendices listing plants by mail, butterfly gardens to visit, butterfly organizations, native plant organizations, and suggestions for further reading. Gorgeous photographs help reveal the life cycle of butterflies as well as the plants required by specific species.

Selsam, Millicent. *Mushrooms*. Morrow, 1986. 48 pp. (P-I). RMA 6.1.
  Black and white photos and simple text tell the history of mushrooms, describe the plant, explain their growth, and introduce a variety of mushrooms.

Selsam, Millicent. *Popcorn*. Morrow, 1976. 48 pp. (P). Photographs by Jerome Wexler. RMA 4.5.
  Selsam describes the life cycle and cultivation of the variety of corn that pops, as well as recounts the history and subsidiary uses of popcorn.

Selsam, Millicent. *The Tomato and Other Fruit Vegetables*. Morrow, 1970. 47 pp. (P). RMA 4.3. Photographs by Jerome Wexler.
  Fruit vegetables? What an odd appellation! But Selsam explains all as she describes the life cycles of green beans, eggplant, peas, and cucumbers. What do they all have in common? They all contain seeds; thus they are the fruit of the plant. Jerome Wexler's 52 clear, close-up photographs help the young botanist get an understandable notion about vegetables that are really fruits.

Selsam, Millicent. *Tree Flowers*. Morrow, 1984. 32 pp. (P-I). Illustrated by Carol Lerner. RMA 6.5.
  Annotations by Selsam provide information about 12 common flowering trees and their botanical parts illustrated by Lerner. The illustrations are of pussywillow, white oak, sugar maple, elm, apple, horse chestnut, dogwood, magnolia, witch hazel, black walnut, black locust, and tulip trees.

Selsam, Millicent. *Where Do They Go? Insects in Winter*. Four Winds, 1982. 32 pp. (P-I). RMA 9.2.
  Poetic text tells where grasshoppers, butterflies, bees, flies, and other common insects spend the winter.

Selsam, Millicent, and Jerome Wexler. *The Amazing Dandelion*. Morrow, 1977. 46 pp. (P-I). RMA 3.3.
  Through Wexler's photographs and Selsam's clear writing the dandelion's life cycle and growing habits are portrayed.

Selsam, Millicent, and Jerome Wexler. *Bulbs, Corms, and Such.* Morrow, 1974. 48 pp. (P-I). RMA 3.2.

Bulbs, corms, rhizomes, and tubers are photographed and described along with explanations about their growing habits.

Selsam, Millicent, and Jerome Wexler. *Mimosa: The Sensitive Plant.* Morrow, 1978. 48 pp. (P). RMA 3.3.

A fascinating, responsive-to-touch plant is revealed in close-up photographs and clear, readable text. The mimosa is called the "sensitive plant" because of its rapid response to heat and touch. This book describes those responses and gives directions for growing the plant.

Shanberg, Karen, and Stan Tekula. *Plantworks.* Adventure Publications, 1991. (I). RMA 1.2.

A wild plant cookbook, field guide, and activity book, this work is intended for the novice naturalist.

Shannon, George. *Seeds.* Houghton Mifflin, 1994. 32 pp. (P). Illustrated by Steve Bjorkman. RMA 2.3.

Warren and Bill have been friends and neighbors for a long time. Warren enjoys Bill's zoo garden. One day Warren's family moves to another town. Warren and Bill miss their visits in the garden. To solve this problem, Bill sends Warren a box of seeds.

Shuttleworth, Floyd S. *Non-Flowering Plants.* Golden Press, 1967. 159 pp. (P-I). RMA 6.2.

Ferns and their related families are the topic of this field guide. A diagram of the life cycle of ferns is included.

Simon, Seymour. *Beneath Your Feet.* Walker, 1977. 44 pp. (P). RMA 7.1.

Simple explanations about and experiments with soil are given.

Simon, Seymour. *A Handful of Soil.* Hawthorn, 1970. 63 pp. (I). RMA 7.1.

More extensive explanations of soil composition and inhabitants are described for the intermediate-grade reader.

Skelsey, Alice, and Gloria Huckaby. *Growing Up Green.* Workman, 1973. 240 pp. (I). RMA 11.2, 11.4.

Although the fashions and the authors' attitudes are quintessentially of the seventies, the text contains highly worthwhile and usable gardening information. Particularly of note are the short biographies of botanists and the accompanying simple science experiments. Latinized scientific names are explained and examples given in the Linnaeus section.

Youthful garden designers will find ideas for various gardens in the "Five Foot Farms" chapter, while those interested in starting plant collections will find helpful hints in the "Cacti, Ferns, Herbs" chapter.

In addition to basic how-to garden information, there are lists of state flowers, birds, and trees as well as the addresses of major plant societies.

Slawson, Michele Benoit, and Deborah Ray. *Apple Picking Time.* Crown, 1994. 32 pp. (P). RMA 5.1.

From dawn to dusk a little girl works alongside her family as they pick apples. Readers hear the story of her day. The author is from the Yakima Valley, a major apple-growing area of Washington.

Smith, Trevor. *Amazing Lizards.* Knopf, 1990. 29 pp. (P-I). RMA 9.3.

Readers learn about chameleons, geckos, horned toads, iguanas, tree dragons, and other lizards in this photographic recounting.

Sobol, Harriet. *A Book of Vegetables.* Dodd, Mead, 1984. 46 pp. (P-I). RMA 4.1, 4.3.

Fourteen vegetables are described. The text conveys the history and uses of each vegetable. This book could be incorporated with a social studies lesson in which a world map is used to trace each of the vegetable's geographical origins. The author and photographer intend for readers to get beyond a grocery store concept of vegetables.

Soucie, Anita H. *Plant Fun: Ten Easy Plants to Grow Indoors.* Four Winds, 1974. 126 pp. (I). RMA 1.1.

Chock-full of good directions and helpful hints for the propagation and care of easy-to-grow house plants, Soucie's book will please the 10- to 12-year-old hobby hunter. Plant lovers can't seem to get enough advice, and this book has plenty to offer. A glossary, index, and symptom-solution chart round out the contents.

Soutter-Perrot, Andrienne. *Earthworm.* Creative Edition, 1993. 32 pp. (P). RMA 9.1.

Simple text and vibrant illustrations depict the earthworm, what it is, where it lives, and how it helps us.

Soutter-Perrot, Andrienne. *The Oak.* Creative Edition, 1993. 32 pp. (P). RMA 6.5.

Simple text with charming, colorful illustrations depict the oak tree: what it is and how it lives, reproduces, and grows.

Souza, D. M. *Insects in the Garden.* Carolrhoda, 1991. 40 pp. (P). RMA 9.2.

With the primary emphasis on beneficial insects, Souza describes common insects found in the garden. Souza divides the insects by their characteristics: high jumpers, invaders, dragons in the sky, and builders.

Sterling, Dorothy. *The Story of Mosses, Ferns, and Mushrooms.* Doubleday, 1955. 159 pp. (I). RMA 6.2

The history of the first plants, algae and mosses, begins about 2 billion years ago. This book traces the world travels and tells the story of early plants, including fungi, mushrooms, ferns, and lichen, which was the manna of the Bible.

Stevenson, Peter, and Mike Stevenson. *Farming in Boxes: One Way to Get Started Growing Things.* Scribner, 1976. 64 pp. (I). RMA 7.3, 11.2.

A garden doesn't have to be a half acre in the middle of a grassy lawn. These boys will show you how to have a garden on macadam lots. A materials list and directions for building the boxes are included .

Stolz, Mary. *The Scarecrows and Their Child.* Harper & Row, 1987. 67 pp. (I). RMA 8.1.

When Handy and Blossom the scarecrows are whisked away to be Halloween decorations, they are separated from their "child," a cat name Bohel. Missing his parents, Bohel sets off to find them and adventure follows. Stolz has written a Halloween fantasy for older boys and girls.

Sunset Editors. *Best Kids Garden Book.* Sunset, 1992. 96 pp. (P-I). RMA 1.5, 5.4, 7.4, 7.5, 8.4.

This comprehensive garden book covers the basics. Readers will learn about gardening tools, planning a garden, starting a worm box, preparing soil, and starting plants from seeds. Cultivation techniques and house plant care are also covered.

T

Tabrah, Ruth, ed. *Momotaro.* Island Heritage, 1992. 60 pp. (I). RMA 5.2.

A young man who began his life in a giant peach saves the family fortune after it is stolen by ogres. A pheasant, a monkey, and a dog assist in this ancient Japanese folktale.

Thaler, Mike. *The Yellow Brick Toad: Funny Frog Cartoons, Riddles, and Silly Stories.* Doubleday, 1978. 96 pp. (P-I). RMA 9.4.

Jokes, riddles, cartoons, and funny stories about frogs and toads will amuse readers.

Thomas, Elizabeth. *Green Beans.* Carolrhoda, 1992. (P-I). RMA 4.1.

Children will enjoy having this story read to them. Grandma's green beans refuse to grow until she goes on vacation. Grandma is one for the rules but she forgets a big one for gardeners: Sometimes you just have to let nature take its course.

Tilgner, Linda. *Let's Grow!* Storey Communications, 1988. 208 pp. (I). **8.4;** RMA 8.2.

Here are 72 garden activities for children. Planting Native American gardens, making corn husk dolls and scarecrows, planting a fruit tree, growing mold gardens, making sunprints, and pressing flowers are just a few of the many lively activities included. Sound gardening advice and instructions are given. The photographs of highly enthusiastic young gardeners motivate readers to try their hand at the projects. Especially worth noting are the suggestions about working with very young children and children with disabilities, such as a physically disabled or developmentally delayed child.

Tillett, Leslie. *Plant and Animal Alphabet Coloring Book.* Dover, 1980. 48 pp. (P-I). RMA 3.4.

This alphabet coloring book based on accurate illustrations will provide a guide to identifying and representing plants and animals.

Trimby, Elisa. *Mr. Plum's Paradise.* Lothrop, Lee & Shepard, 1976. 32 pp. (P). RMA 11.5.

Mr. Plum dreams of and plants a beautiful flower garden in the backyard of his city row house. His neighbors, upon seeing how beautiful it is, want to knock down the walls and turn their backyards into one large community garden.

Turner, Dorothy. *Potatoes.* Carolrhoda, 1989. 32 pp. (P). Illustrated by John Yates. RMA 4.4.

This book describes the history, cultivation, and nutritional value of potatoes. Craft projects and recipes are included.

V

Van Allsburg, Christopher. *Just a Dream.* Houghton Mifflin, 1990. 48 pp. (I). RMA 8.5.

Walter, who is clueless and indifferent about caring for the environment, is transformed by a dream. He wakes up literally and figuratively and changes his habits.

Velghe, Anne. *Wildflowers: A Primer.* Farrar, Straus & Giroux, 1994. 32 pp. (P). RMA 3.5.

Uncaptioned watercolors of various wildflowers and children are portrayed. Each wildflower is identified by a number. Explanations follow on the next pages.

W

Wadsworth, Olive. *Over in the Meadow.* Puffin Books, 1985. 31 pp. (P). Illustrations by Mary Maki Rae. RMA 10.4.

The old counting-out rhyme is given new bounce with Rae's warm illustrations. This is one of several counting books in this bibliography, the others being McMillan's *Counting Wildflowers* and Lottridge's *One Watermelon Seed.* Connections to math are encouraged.

Walker, Lois. *Get Growing! Exciting Indoor Plant Projects for Kids.* Wiley, 1991. 102 pp. (P-I). RMA 1.3.

Directions are given for growing carrots, citrus seeds, beans, potatoes, pineapples, peanuts, avocados, and mangos, popcorn, sprouts, tomatoes, and apples. Instructions for crafts and recipes related to each plant are also provided. Grow a carrot upside down, write a secret message with invisible lemon juice ink, make pineapple pine cones, create a glass-jar greenhouse, or make applehead puppets—these are only several of the projects likely to engage the interest of children.

Walters, Jennie. *Gardening with Peter Rabbit.* Warne, 1992. 46 pp. (P-I). RMA 1.5, 4.3, 11.1.

Divided by the seasons, the text provides directions for 20 garden-related projects. Many of these projects may be found in other books; one that is different from all others is the blossoming branch in which a split bamboo branch is used to support marigold or nasturtium plants.

Waters, Marjorie. *The Victory Garden Kids' Book.* Globe Pequot, 1994. 148 pp. (I). **11.2;** RMA 4.1, 4.3, 7.3, 7.4, 8.4, 11.5.

A comprehensive book about gardening for and with children, the text conveys information about site selection, soil testing, soil preparation, planting, weeding, harvesting, and preparing the garden plot for winter. Sidebars tell of crops for different climates, buying seedlings, and window box gardening. The book includes excellent sections about composting, measuring rain, beneficial insects, and how to grow the biggest pumpkin. The second half of the book describes individual vegetables and flowers from basil to zucchini. A special feature of this book is "The Yardstick Garden." In every chapter Waters provides information about constructing and caring for a 3′-x-3′ garden that is planned step by step for beginning gardeners.

Watts, Barrie. *Mushroom.* Silver Burdett, 1986. 24 pp. (P). RMA 6.1.

Clear color photos, simple text, and diagrams describe the growth of mushrooms.

Watts, Barrie. *Potato.* Silver Burdett, 1988. 25 pp. (P-I). RMA 4.4.

Primarily the story is told through photographs. A potato's life cycle is shown from planting to blossoming to harvest. Watts cautions readers not to eat the potato fruit because it is poisonous. Cut-away drawings show the edible tubers growing underground.

Watts, Barrie. *Tomato.* Silver Burdett, 1990. 24 pp. (P). **4.3.**

Vivid color photography brings the reader into close-up contact with tomato plants, flowers, fruit, and seeds. The tomato life cycle is shown in step-by-step photographic sequence throughout the book. From seed to harvest, close-up photographs and drawings explain to the young readers how a tomato grows. The author wants his book read by several ages. He puts important information in boldface print and simple language for the beginning reader and provides more detailed descriptions for the second-grade reader.

Watts, Claire, and Alexandra Parson. *Make It Work! Plants.* Macmillan, 1993. 48 pp. (P-I). Photography by Jon Barnes. RMA 2.1.

Art and science are combined in projects designed to help children comprehend botany concepts and processes. A very attractive book with fun ideas, it is sure to capture children's interests.

Webster, David. *Exploring Nature Around the Year: Fall.* Messner, 1989. 48 pp. (I). **1.2.**

This book is one of a series of four that encourages readers to explore seasonal changes in the natural world. Pictures, diagrams, and readable text present information and activities. Fall explorations feature leaves, apples, seeds, soil, birds, and animals as well as the sky. The final project is to create a nature museum.

Wexler, Jerome. *From Spore to Spore: Ferns and How They Grow.* Dodd, Mead, 1985. 48 pp. (P-I). **6.2.**

Wexler's text conveys information about the fern's life cycle and gives advice on cultivating ferns.

Wexler, Jerome. *Jack-in-the-Pulpit.* Dutton, 1993. 38 pp. (P-I). RMA 3.5.

Glistening close-up photographs show readers the life cycle of a favorite wildflower. The text provides ample information for the young botanist. Gorgeous!

Wexler, Jerome. *Queen Anne's Lace.* Whitman, 1994. 32 pp. (P-I). RMA 3.5.

Wexler explains the intricacies of the habitat, characteristics, and life cycle of this favorite, ubiquitous flower. His photographs, panoramic and up close, support the text so the reader sees the plant within the context of its habitat as well as the details of its structure. Botanical vocabulary is embedded and explained throughout the text, as it is in the books he writes alone and in partnership with Selsam. After a number of these books are read by children, they should be able to pick up the technical vocabulary of plants naturally without a lot of direct instruction.

Wexler, Jerome. *Secrets of the Venus's Fly Trap.* Dodd Mead, 1981. 64 pp. (P-I). RMA 6.4.

Wexler provides experiments and answers about the food, structure, propagation, and care of this insectivorous plant.

Wexler, Jerome. *Sundew Stranglers: Plants That Eat Insects.* Dutton, 1995. 46 pp. (I). **6.4.**

Fascinating reading even if the idea of insect-eating plants leaves you cold. Wexler's clear explanations and close-up photographs draw the reader into the explanations, experiments, and history of a plant variety that grows on every continent except Antarctica. Readers will discover the mechanism by which the sundew captures and digests insects. Wexler tells his readers that sundews are easy to grow and tells how to do that. He advises readers to contact the carnivorous plant association: The International Carnivorous Plant Society, Fullerton Arboretum, California State University, Fullerton, CA 92634.

Wexler, Jerome. *Wonderful Pussy Willows.* Dutton, 1992. 32 pp. (P-I). RMA 6.5.

Highly magnified time-lapse photographs show the reproductive cycle of the pussy willow. Readers learn technical vocabulary within the context of clear explanations and brilliant photographs.

Wiesner, David. *Tuesday.* Clarion, 1991. 32 pp. (P-I). RMA 9.4.

Wiesner's droll fantasy of frogs that are transported on their lily pads into the world of suburbia delights children and adults. Adults will have no difficulty getting apprentice writers and readers to produce very humorous stories when they use this mostly wordless book.

Wilkes, Angela. *Growing Things.* Usborne House, 1984. 24 pp. (P). RMA 11.3.

Wilkes demonstrates step-by-step instructions and practical tips for growing flowers, trees, herbs, and vegetables for very young readers.

Wilkes, Angela. *My First Garden Book.* Knopf, 1992. 48 pp. (P-I). RMA 1.1, 2.4, 11.1.

Restricted to indoor plants, this book conveys information primarily through photographs.

Wilkes, Angela. *My First Green Book.* Knopf, 1991. 48 pp. (P-I). RMA 10.5.

Wilkes presents activities and experiments about the importance of green plants to earth's oxygen supply. She describes how to create a wildlife garden.

Wilkins, Verna, and Gill McLean. *Five Things to Find.* Tamarind, 1991. 24 pp. (P). RMA 8.3.

In this retold Tunisian folktale, Hassan, Yasmin, and Fatima are told by their father to find five special things within three days. The father urges them to work as a team. However, while Hassan and Yasmin scurry about searching, Fatima sits still and ponders the problem. She succeeds in finding exactly what her father requested.

Williams, Vera B. *Cherries and Cherry Pits.* Greenwillow, 1986. 36 pp. (P). **5.3.**

Bidemmi loves to color; she loves to draw; she loves to tell stories. With her markers she draws pictures about which she begins to tell stories with the word "This." She draws pictures and tells stories about people who like to eat cherries. Her last story is about herself planting the cherry pits that will sprout into trees. As Bidemmi says, "I know that if I plant enough of them, at least one cherry tree will grow." Bidemmi imagines the future with all her friends enjoying her cherry "forest."

This book is perfect for youth leaders, teachers, and librarians looking for a way to motivate students to write. They may be encouraged to start their stories just as Bidemmi did, with "This."

Often in gardening and botany classes, students are asked to draw a series of pictures showing what is occurring to a plant over time. Bidemmi shows kids how to do this.

Wilner, Isabel. *A Garden Alphabet.* Dutton, 1991. 32 pp. (P). RMA 3.4.

Frog and dog, two good gardening friends, demonstrate gardening events. The reader is taken throughout the season as well as the alphabet.

Wood, Don, and Audrey Wood. *The Little Mouse, the Red Ripe Strawberry and the Big Hungry Bear.* Child's Play, 1984. 32 pp. (P). RMA 5.4.

A mouse is persuaded to try many ways to disguise and hide a strawberry from a bear, only to be fooled, as the reader may be also.

Woodside, Dave. *What Makes Popcorn Pop?* Atheneum, 1980. 74 pp. (I). RMA 4.5.

The history, lore, and little-known facts about popcorn are presented along with its cultivation and a few recipes.

Woolfit, Gabrielle. *Sow and Grow.* Thompson Learning, 1994. 32 pp. (P-I). RMA 2.4.

Twelve plant and garden projects are described. These include designing a floral display garden, growing potatoes in pots, and planting an herb garden in a container. The medicinal uses of plants are described, making this book a good companion to Dowden's *Poisons in Our Path*. A bibliography of other garden books is included. Children from diverse populations are depicted.

Wyler, Rose. *Science Fun with Mud and Dirt*. Messner, 1986. 48 pp. (P-I). **7.1.**

In easy-to-understand text, the structure and composition of dirt are detailed. Experiments and projects with dirt are described, as are dirt's inhabitants. Wyler explains the importance of soil to human life and encourages children to conserve it.

Y

Yolen, Jane. *Bird Watch*. Philomel, 1991. 48 pp. (P-I). RMA 10.2.

A collection of 17 poems celebrates birds and displays them in their natural habitats through poetry and art.

Yolen, Jane. *Elfabet: An ABC of Elves*. Little, Brown, 1990. 32 pp. (P). RMA 3.4.

Each letter is represented by a busy elf surrounded by a myriad of brightly hued birds, flowers, and animals.

Z

Zagwyn, Deborah. *The Pumpkin Blanket*. Celestial Arts, 1990. 32 pp. (P). RMA 4.2.

Clee has grown attached to her patchwork quilt. It has brought joy and comfort to her childhood. Her father needs the patches to protect the pumpkins from frost. Clee gives her blanket, patch by patch, to save the pumpkins.

Zimmelman, Nathan. *I Will Tell You of Peach Stone*. Lothrop, Lee & Shepard, 1976. 26 pp. (P). Illustrated by Haru Wells. RMA 5.2.

As the old storyteller and his dog Peach Stone live through a lonely winter, they decide to embark on a journey in order to take peaches to a land where the peach tree does not grow. A story about the virtue of bringing good things to where they are needed.

Zion, Gene. *The Plant Sitter*. Harper, 1959. 26 pp. (P). RMA 1.1.

Tommy, an entrepreneur, offered a plant-sitting service for the neighbors, much to the dismay of his parents. He took such good care of the plants that they became overgrown. Tommy consulted a library book and learned how to make cuttings. These he gave to his friends.

Activities Index

Creative Activities

Gardening Activities

Language Arts Activity

Treats

Author/Title/Subject Index

Listed here are those books and authors mentioned in the text as well as general subjects. Numbers in bold refer to lesson numbers. For a full listing of authors and books used for the lessons, refer to the annotated bibliography.

About the Authors

Nancy Allen Jurenka

With this book, two lifelong interests of Nancy Allen Jurenka, children's literature and gardening, have been brought together. Among her childhood recollections is helping her father plant his gladiola garden, followed months later by the enchantment of harvesting, what seemed to her, a rainbow in a basket. Her own first garden achievement was the patch of marigolds and zinnias that she planted to receive her Home Gardener Girl Scout badge. Today, she gardens at Book Nook Farm and teaches children's literature at Central Washington University in Ellensburg, Washington, where she is Assistant Professor. She is the co-author of *Responding to Literature: Activities for Grades 6, 7, 8* (Englewood, CO: Teacher Ideas Press, 1991).

She can vouch that starting a child off in life with these two interests, books and plants, will result in a lifetime of pleasure. "Cicero got it right," she claims, 'If you have a garden and a library, you have everything you need.'"

Rosanne Johnson Blass

Rosanne Blass is a Visiting Professor in the College of Education at the University of South Florida, St. Petersburg. Dr. Blass completed her master's and doctoral degrees at the University of Tennessee after receiving her bachelor's degree at the University of Minnesota. Her experience includes teaching in public, private, and parochial schools in Minnesota, Michigan, Tennessee, Pennsylvania, Ohio, California, Arizona, and Florida. She is the co-author of *Responding to Literature: Activities for Grades 6, 7, 8* (Englewood, CO: Teacher Ideas Press, 1991).

from Teacher Ideas Press

CULTIVATING A CHILD'S IMAGINATION THROUGH GARDENING
Nancy Allen Jurenka and Rosanne J. Blass

Each of these 45 lessons focuses on a specific book about gardening and offers related activities such as reading, writing, poetry, word play, music, dancing, dramatics, and other activities to enhance creativity and build literacy skills. A great companion to *Beyond the Bean Seed*. **Grades K–6**.
Due: Fall 1996 ca.125p. 8½x11 paper ISBN 1-56308-452-X

EXPLORATIONS IN BACKYARD BIOLOGY:
Drawing on Nature in the Classroom, Grades 4–6
R. Gary Raham, Illustrated by the author

Use these hands-on science explorations for exciting classroom and field activities. Through drawing and writing students record their experiences in a Naturalist's Notebook, which facilitates further discoveries. **Grades 4–6**.
Due: Spring 1996 ca.250p. 8½x11 paper ISBN 1-56308-254-3

SCIENCE THROUGH CHILDREN'S LITERATURE: An Integrated Approach
Carol M. Butzow and John W. Butzow

Instructional units integrate all areas of the curriculum and serve as models to educators at all levels. Adopted by schools of education nationwide, this book features more than 30 outstanding children's fiction books that are rich in scientific concepts yet equally well known for their strong story lines and universal appeal. **Grades K–3**.
xviii, 234p. 8½x11 paper ISBN 0-87287-667-5

INTERMEDIATE SCIENCE THROUGH CHILDREN'S LITERATURE:
Over Land and Sea
Carol M. Butzow and John W. Butzow

Focusing on earth and environmental science themes and activities for intermediate grades, this book covers such topics as oceans, lakes, rivers, mountain formations, air, weather, the tundra, deserts, fossils, plant and animal interdependence, and environmental quality. Hands-on and discovery activities span all disciplines of the middle school curriculum. **Grades 4–7**.
xxv, 193p. 8½x11 paper ISBN 0-87287-946-1

RAINY, WINDY, SNOW, SUNNY DAYS: Linking Fiction to Nonfiction
Phyllis J. Perry

Help students make the transition from fiction to nonfiction reading. This book offers summaries of children's literature and nonfiction books related to weather—rain, wind, snow, and sunshine—then suggests books which combine elements of both. **Grades K–5**.
Literature Bridges to Science Series
xiii, 147p. 8½x11 paper ISBN 1-56308-392-2

MATH THROUGH CHILDREN'S LITERATURE:
Making the NCTM Standards Come Alive
Kathryn L. Braddon, Nancy J. Hall, and Dale Taylor

Following the NCTM Standards, this book uses children's literature as a springboard to help teachers lead children along the path to successful mathematical literacy. Activities and summaries of books, each related to the standards, help children gain familiarity with and an understanding of mathematical concepts. **Grades 1–6**.
xviii, 218p. 8½x11 paper ISBN 0-87287-932-1

ONE VOICE: Music and Stories in the Classroom
Barbara M. Britsch and Amy Dennison-Tansey

This treasury of improvisational music and drama, child-centered art, child-created story productions, and other outstanding activities emphasizes participation and helps students experience the imaginative possibilities of music and storytelling. **Grades K–6**.
xxiv, 175p. 8½x11 paper ISBN 1-56308-049-4

For a free catalog or to order these or any other TIP titles, please contact:
Teacher Ideas Press • Dept. B8 • P.O. Box 6633 • Englewood, CO 80155
Phone: 1-800-237-6124, ext. 1 • Fax: 1-303-220-8843 • E-mail: lu-books@lu.com